"A detailed and informative discussion on the elusive subject of greenscreening, full of tips and techniques that any compositing artist can use to improve their work. The book's holistic approach towards getting a better key, as well as its excellent overview of the third-party tools that can help you do it even better, make this compendium an essential guide to convincingly place your subject in another environment."
Aharon Rabinowitz, Creative Director, All Bets Are Off Productions

"This is an amazing book! This book belongs right next to Stu Maschwitz's *DV Rebels Guide* as an additional tool in your reference arsenal. The topics covered here leave you with no questions and conjecture about how to shoot, light, and pull the perfect key. This is probably the most comprehensive information I have seen that really covers this often-discussed topic."
Seth Hancock, Executive Producer & On-air Talent, WXIN-TV

"Greenscreen techniques have long been the most secretive and important aspect of special effects work. This guide elucidates the topic better than any I have yet seen."
Mason Dixon, Motion Graphics Festival & School of the Art Institute of Chicago. *www.MGFest.com*

"I recently finished writing on a TV series that was shot almost entirely on a green-screen, and when I began, I had no idea what terms like "rotoscoping" and "mask" actually meant. If I'd had this book at the beginning, I could've learned that stuff in a single read... rather than semi-absorbing it over several months. And while greenscreen is still a highly technical, often daunting world, Jeremy Hanke and Michele Yamazaki make it simple and digestible even to idiots like me, non-techies who would much rather be sitting at a desk writing jokes or outlining stories. So whether you're the post guy actually running After Effects... or just a writer/director/actor/producer who wants to understand what's going on at other stages of the project, this is a current, relevant and easy-to-read guide you don't want to miss."
Chad Gervich, TV Writer/Producer and Author of *Small Screen, Big Picture: A Writer's Guide to the TV Business*

"Comprehensive, easy to read, and relates to not only beginners but those of us who have wrestled with the effective use of greenscreening for years. We are going to recommend this to both our film and TV production students. I have tried a few of the light suggestions and was surprised how useful they were. This is a must for students, independents, and working pros who want good results!"
Mark Kruhmin, Television Production Specialist, Saddleback College

"In the Swiss Army knife of production, this book sits right next to the *DV Rebels Guide* as the bone saw and screwdriver — necessary tools for any job. The way the information is presented is engaging and easy to process while still being extremely informative and technical. In a word, this book is *essential*."
Jason Diamond, Co-owner/Co-Founder of MBS Productions (MTV, VH1, Spike TV)

"In the digital filmmaking age of this decade, I've shot many music videos and short subjects in front of greenscreen, keying out the green in Final Cut Pro.... Oh, how I wish that I had *Greenscreen Made Easy* as a reference guide BEFORE I had created these projects!!! An excellent tool for beginners and novice filmmakers!"
  Scott Essman, VISIONARY CINEMA

"A thorough, well-researched, and clearly illustrated book. *Greenscreen Made Easy* is the essential reference for turning out low-budget, high-production-value movies. Page after page of information no filmmaker can do without.
  Jerome Olivier, Writer, Director, Producer, Missing Pages

"From shooting to postproduction, this book not only helps you to understand green-screening, but also teaches you to apply it correctly to your project. A must-have book for students, filmmakers, and animators alike."
  Dru Nget, Designer/Animator, Shine (*Kung Fu Panda, Traitor, Mad Money*)

"*Greenscreen Made Easy* is the definitive book on low-budget chromakeying. The chapter on building your own greenscreen studio is absolutely invaluable for DIY indie filmmakers, and the lighting chapter is easily the most comprehensive I've seen on the subject. If I'd had this book when I was making my feature film, I literally would have saved myself hundreds of hours in research, on-set trial and error, and postproduction nightmares."
  Ryan Graham, Writer/Director (*Livelihood*), 37.5 Studios

"*Greenscreen Made Easy* contains everything you could ever need to know about how to create a great composite. They've included absolutely everything! From creating your own green/bluescreen, to shooting background elements that match, to lighting, this contains everything you need to know about this subject. And it explains the whole process in a way that's easy to follow and interesting. I wish I could have read this book before I made my first feature!"
  Cindy Baer, Award-winning Director (*Purgatory House, Morbid Curiosity*)

"*Greenscreen Made Easy* is an invaluable tool for the independent filmmaker, pulling back the curtain on tricks of the trade and putting them right into the hands of the microbudget auteur. I wish I had a resource like this when I started making movies, and I'm thrilled to have it as I continue."
  Mike Flanagan, Award-winning Filmmaker (*Oculus, The Ghosts of Hamilton Street, Still Life*), Mike Flanagan Films

If you have ever wondered if you could pull off your own visual effects on a budget, wonder no more. *Greenscreen Made Easy* is a practical handbook written for real people. The tips from affordable cameras and green-screen equipment to a ton of Adobe After Effects techniques make this book downright crafty. Lights, camera, green-screen compositing!
  Dan Rosen, Visual Effects Supervisor & Owner of Evil Eye Pictures — feature film credits include *The Matrix* Trilogy, *Pirates of the Caribbean 2 & 3, Spider-Man 3, Speed Racer,* and *Australia*

GREENSCREEN MADE EASY
KEYING AND COMPOSITING
FOR INDIE FILMMAKERS

BY
JEREMY HANKE
& MICHELE YAMAZAKI

MICHAEL WIESE PRODUCTIONS

Published by Michael Wiese Productions
3940 Laurel Canyon Blvd. – Suite 1111
Studio City, CA 91604
(818) 379-8799, (818) 986-3408 (FAX).
mw@mwp.com
www.mwp.com

Cover design by MWP
Interior design by William Morosi
Copyedited by Bob Somerville
Printed by Sheridan Books, Inc.

Manufactured in the United States of America
Copyright 2009

Library of Congress Cataloging-in-Publication Data

Hanke, Jeremy, 1977–
  GreenScreen made easy / Jeremy Hanke & Michele Yamazaki. -- 2nd ed.
    p. cm.
  Includes bibliographical references and index.
  ISBN 978-1-932907-54-4 (alk. paper)
  1. Cinematography--Special effects. I. Yamazaki, Michele, 1973- II. Title.
  TR858.H3525 2009
  778.5'345--dc22
                          2008038632

TABLE OF CONTENTS

Chapters 1-10 by Jeremy Hanke
Chapters 11-19 by Michele Yamazaki

ACKNOWLEDGMENTS

Special photos, artwork, footage, and information provided by: Adobe, Artemis Pictures, Panasonic, ARRI, Divergent Media, *Micro-Filmmaker* Magazine, Zylight, David Torno, Ralph Caldwell, Sam Fisher, Toby Gaines, Angie Mistretta, and Tom Stern.

Special thanks to: Tom Stern for his brilliant research and extremely helpful video footage and composited pictures; Paul Babb, the president of Cinema 4D, for his help with getting us useful information for the 3D section of the book.

CHAPTER 1: WHAT IS CHROMAKEYING?

If you've picked up this book, you've probably been fascinated by the effects work you've seen in Hollywood films, in everything from *The Matrix* to *The Lord of the Rings* to *Sin City*. All of these films use chromakeying to realize some element of the storytelling process that the filmmaker wanted to show but that could not be shot in a normal, real-world environment. To be able to magically place your actors into steaming jungles, science fiction metropolises, or ultragritty city streets has been a pursuit of filmmakers since Florey and Vorkapich's *The Life and Death of 9413, a Hollywood Extra* and Fritz Lang's *Metropolis* experimented with stationary mattes. These early filmmakers used cut mattes to block a section of the exposure of the film negative and then used reversals of these mattes to expose only those sections to alternate scenes. Because these early effects combined portions of two scenes, they were the first composites. Later, motion mattes were utilized during the filming of movies like *Mary Poppins*, which allowed a background to be removed from behind a moving actor. These motion mattes were actually the first form of chromakeying.

So what exactly is chromakeying? Many of us find the term "chromakeying" to be a bit daunting. Even the name is a little confusing, as it sounds like something you'd pay to have done to a classic '57 Chevy's bumpers. Of course, it becomes at least a little more familiar to us when it's boiled down to its most popular derivative in this neo-digital age: "greenscreening."

I've done a lot of research into this subject as I've prepared for this book, but I'm hard pressed to come up with a more concise description of the technology than the one given by effects filmmaker Zach from Fox's *On the Lot*: "Greenscreening is just basically telling the camera to replace anything it sees as green with whatever you [the director] want."

So where exactly does the term "chromakeying" come from? In technical terms, "chroma" is the word used to describe color that a camera can record. ("Luma," on the other hand, describes the light that a camera can record.) "Keying" is an old production term that refers to removing an object from a picture using a form of matte. So chromakeying is simply removing any color that you designate and creating a matte in the shape of the removed color. (This is especially appropriate because chromakeying didn't start out with the color green, or even the second most popular color — blue — for that matter. *Mary Poppins* utilized a yellow background behind the actors.) Over these matted-out areas, the keying or editing software you use shows any background you choose.

(Because of the prevalence of the term "chromakeying" in the television industry, we will simply refer to this concept as "greenscreening" to prevent confusion.)

Just because we know the general science behind greenscreen technology, however, doesn't make the creation of truly convincing greenscreen effects any less mysterious. It's all well and good to realize that you shoot something or someone in front of a colored background that is different from your subject and that you can have almost any editor or keyer delete the background. But anyone who's dabbled in this strangely occult field has probably discovered that their results often don't hold a candle to the work done by ILM or TroubleMaker Studios.

When you try greenscreening and don't get great results, it can be really tempting to just write it off as something that you're not able to do in a believable way on a low budget. Hollywood studios have extremely powerful equipment, software, and a lot of money to make their movie magic, so it can be easy to believe that their advantage allows them to do what we cannot. As we were preparing for this book, we looked at the most common hurdles facing low-budget filmmakers seeking good-quality greenscreen results.

The number one hurdle was simply a lack of readily available information on the art of greenscreening. Aside from some work by Creative Cow and Andrew Kramer, until recently information for the low-budget filmmaker on the art of greenscreening has been minimal. Lots of filmmakers had to strike out on their own and try to get something that looked halfway decent, hoping they would happen upon the right blend of color, lighting, camera quality, and keying software to get what they were aiming for. While some folks have succeeded in this area by teaching themselves, many more have given up after being unable to harness the technology. This past year, more magazines have looked at greenscreening and at least one other book on the art of greenscreening has been released. However, most of these resources put a greater focus on surrealistic, as opposed to realistic, greenscreening. The art of greenscreening a weathercaster or someone in front of a digital background for an infomercial is not the same as the art of greenscreening a protagonist into a 3D temple and making it believable. In the weather and infomercials, everyone knows it's all computer-generated and they don't care. But in feature films you've got to convince the audience that your actor is really in the location you're showing. Low-budget feature-film greenscreen is the most profound magic show on the planet. You have to be more deft with sleight of hand than Hollywood does, because you just don't have the budget to do things the way Hollywood does them.

This chapter is designed to give you some understanding of how to recognize the limitations low-budget filmmakers face in terms of their equipment, because only by understanding your limitations can you learn how to overcome them.

To explain why many of us have had frustrating results when it comes to greenscreening, we must start with the fact that we have been working with suboptimal source material.

What do I mean by suboptimal? DV, HDV, and even most HD footage is suboptimal. This is due to how DV, HDV, and HD cameras that are affordable record light (luma) and color (chroma) information. (The only exception to this is the new RED camera, which is only affordable because Jim Jannard, the president of RED, is already the multi-millionaire owner of Oakley Sunglasses and doesn't mind creating a Hollywood-quality digital camera for about 10% to 15% of the cost of competing cameras. The $30,000 start-up price is still outside most of our readers' pocketbooks,

Most of our readers will be shooting with color-compressed cameras, like SD, HDV, and HD cameras. So we'll show you how to overcome their limitations as much as possible.

but it's a massive stride in the right direction compared to its $250,000 to $300,000 competitors.)

Color information takes up a lot of bandwidth but is not as noticeable to the human eye as light data is. When DV camera manufacturers were playing lifeboat with different pieces of information for the recording and compression codecs used in these cameras, they decided to record every pixel of light their cameras' sensors picked up, but only *one* out of four pixels recorded color data for NTSC DV cameras.

4:1:1 (NTSC DV) Sampling

Key:
○ = **Luminance** (Brightness) Info
◎ = **Chrominance** (Color) Info

Note: Although circles symbolize pixels in this diagram, actual pixels are square in shape.

As you can see, SD sampling records only one pixel of color information for every four pixels of luminance information.

This was called "4:1:1" color space, with the "4" denoting that four out of four pixels of light information would be recorded, the first "1" denoting that one out of four pixels would have color information recorded in the first line, and the last "1" denoting that one out of four pixels would have color information recorded in the second line. From here, the information is compressed, but luckily each frame is compressed separately.

PAL DV cameras (and now HDV cameras) record with a 4:2:0 color space, which, again, records four out of four light pixels but records color information on two out of four pixels of the first line, and *no* color information on the second line. PAL DV compresses each frame separately, just like NTSC DV.

However, in order for HDV to fit on a single tape, multiple frames must be grouped together and compressed in clusters of between 7 and 15 frames

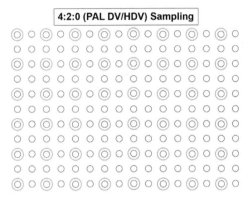

Although PAL and HDV sampling seem to record twice as much color information, this is only true on every other line. The other lines have no color information recorded.

True HD cameras, like the Panasonic HVX200, do record twice as much color information as SD, with every other pixel recording color data.

(7 for JVC and 15 for Sony.) Obviously, when you mash groups of frames together and then must untangle them before you can even begin to key them, this makes getting good keys harder.

HD cameras include everything from Panasonic's HVX200A all the way to compressed Viper footage, and they have a 4:2:2 color space. Again, four out of four pixels have their light data recorded, while every other pixel has its color data recorded in both the first and second line. The footage is compressed before being recorded to the hard drive or tape, but like DV, each frame is compressed individually, which means that there is less damage done by the compression.

What's the color space in those high-end cameras that Robert Rodriguez used to shoot *Sin City*? Uncompressed 4:4:4. That means that every pixel is recorded for both light and color and recorded without compression to a RAID array. Obviously, this gives you optimal chromakeying latitude, as the keying program isn't trying to guess where pixels are because of insufficient color information. (The aforementioned RED camera generates the same color space, provided its uncompressed REDcode RAW stream is recorded.)

For most of us, 4:4:4 is not something we will likely have access to until the RED drops further in price, we sell one of our films for a substantial profit, or we try to hijack the signal from our cameras before its color information gets decimated. (Believe it or not, a company called Real Stream has a $2,500 adapter that they will install in a DVX100 or HVX200A camera so that you can download uncompressed 4:4:4 data directly from the camera's imagers. Unfortunately, the program that reads this data stream is only available for Macs and is reportedly extremely unwieldy to use. Hopefully, in the future, the adapters will come with a cross-platform package that has the kinks worked out.)

Obviously, I don't tell you all these things about greenscreen technology to make you feel like you have to save up until you have a 4:4:4 uncompressed camera in order to start learning it. Instead, I tell you these things so that you understand why special steps need to be taken to get the best keys out of lower-end cameras. From that perspective, we will discuss how to either purchase or build the best type of greenscreen for your needs, and then we will look at how to light both it and your actors properly, how to shoot it cleanly, how to key it with one of the programs that works well with DV/HDV/HD footage, and finally how to composite your keyed footage with both real and 3D generated elements.

Buckle up. This is going to be a wild ride.

CHAPTER 2: TO BUY OR TO BUILD A GREENSCREEN

O kay, to briefly recap the ending of the last chapter, we assume that one of your grandparents hasn't recently left you a large inheritance to purchase one of Robert Rodriguez's cameras — or even a medium-sized inheritance to purchase a new RED one. This means that you'll likely be doing your shooting with a 4:1:1 camera like the Panasonic DVX100, a 4:2:0 camera like the Sony HVR-Z1U, or a 4:2:2 camera like the Panasonic HVX200A.

With that in mind, how do you start on the right foot to make sure you get clean keys in post?

To help ensure success, it is imperative to start with the best possible greenscreen you can either afford or construct. Once you have it, of course, you'll want to light it, position it, and treat it properly, but we'll cover those facets in later chapters.

Now, before we go into whether to buy or to build a greenscreen, let's consider the following question, which invariably pops up: Should it in fact be a green screen or, instead, should it be a blue screen? As the terms appear to be practically interchangeable in every DVD extra you watch — and even in many special effects books — it's hard to keep track of who uses which color for what purposes. Even professionals seem to get glib on this subject. To illustrate what I mean, one of our staff writers was on an industry tour of a Hollywood studio and one of the other people in the group asked the guide what the difference between greenscreen and bluescreen really was. The guide snidely responded, "Well sir, bluescreens are blue, and greenscreens are green."

So, what is the difference, then? Well, the choice of color is based on two factors: the color of the clothing, hair, or eyes of the person being recorded, and the medium that is doing the recording.

Obviously, if the talent has blue clothing, a greenscreen is the correct choice, and vice versa. Much less obviously, though, hair color has a direct bearing on screen choice. (And no, we're not talking about our friendly neighborhood punks who have dyed their hair literally blue or green.) Blond hair has a way of picking up green that makes it very difficult to key properly from a greenscreen, which is why it has always been customary to film blond actors in front of bluescreens. If your actors don't have blond hair and are wearing neither blue nor green, you will normally look to what you're recording on. Film's blue latitude is excellent, which is why bluescreen was the most intelligent choice for people recording to film. But in digital recording, more green data is recorded (especially in lower-priced cameras like the ones you're using, which discard more information from the red and blue channels). This means that, for most of our readers, greenscreen is often the best choice.

This doesn't mean that the bluescreen concept gets thrown out entirely for digital filmmakers, even if you're not shooting blonds or actors with green clothes (or bright green eyes) in your film. Digital video cameras can still get a very usable key from bluescreens, and it is actually easier to make the color blue really pop with inexpensive lights (which tends to make it more distinct from your foreground subject and, therefore, easier to key). And, of course, for films that are going to have a stylistic blue-tinted final color pass or that are using water and/or cloud-based effects, it's better to use blue. (For example, *Evan Almighty*, which includes massive flood effects, utilized bluescreens successfully because of the blue coloration of the water.) An added benefit of bluescreen is that if you end up with some spill (color reflected onto your actor from the background) that can't be removed in post, blue is less noticeable to the human eye than green. You should at least play around a bit with bluescreen and see if it does what you need for your film.

Since green is still going to be the color that's going to work for many of our readers most of the time, for simplicity we will simply refer to all color-keying technology as "greenscreen" unless we are referring to an actual *blue* screen.

So now we get into the question of whether you should purchase or build your greenscreen. There is no one right answer, but certain factors can help you decide.

The first factor is what you're going to be using greenscreen technology to do. Are you going to use it to delete a few buildings, trucks, or light poles from an otherwise usable shot? Or are you going to completely get rid of all naturally occurring landscape? In the former case, you're typically going to want to buy a collapsible greenscreen, because, as the name implies, collapsible greenscreens are designed to be taken down and put up quickly and with minimal hassle, which makes them ideal for removing a few background elements but leaving the rest of the environment intact. (*The Lord of the Rings* trilogy is a great example; sky and other elements were covered up with portable greenscreens, while the rest of the environment was filmed as is.) If you want to completely remove all natural elements, you're probably going to need to build a greenscreen studio of some sort. Although there are some companies that will build professional greenscreen studios for you, the cost is likely going to be outside your price range. That means you'll have to put in the elbow grease yourself. But when you're done, you'll be able to place your actors in virtually any environment, from outer space to Discworld and everywhere in between (as exemplified in Robert Rodriguez's *Sin City*).

A second factor is whether you want greenscreen to be a small part of one film or a permanent component of your filmmaking repertoire. If your use will be minimal, a purchased, collapsible greenscreen is a great choice; it's not terribly expensive and won't take up much space when you're not using it. But if you're planning to do a lot of greenscreen work, you should seriously consider building a greenscreen studio — and ideally getting a collapsible greenscreen as well.

You have other options beyond these basic rules of thumb. For example, you can patch together a few purchased portable greenscreens to create a greenscreen studio, or you can make your own foam-and-paint portable greenscreen to remove unwanted background segments. (In fact, the movie *Dirty Trousers* — more on which later — used a number of such makeshift greenscreens for just this purpose.)

Now let's get into the options for both purchased and built greenscreen setups.

CHAPTER 3: POPULAR OPTIONS FOR PURCHASING A GREENSCREEN

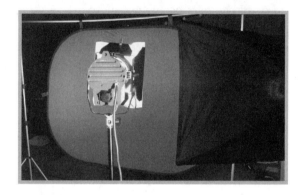

If you can afford them and they suit your needs, buying greenscreens is usually your best bet. Their professionally treated coloration makes it easier to get a uniform key off them. Different manufacturers offer slightly different shades of green (and blue); you'll want to go with a darker shade to guard against overlighting problems. Overlighting happens more often with greenscreens than many people think, and the lighter the shade of green, the easier it is to wash out the color and make the greenscreen harder to key. A darker shade of green gives you more latitude before you start washing out the color.

With that said, let's look at the available options.

Rolled cloth backdrop and stand

The rolled cloth and stand can be a great fit for many low-budget filmmakers, because it's fairly portable and can usually be rolled out to go under the actors' feet, thus creating a cyclorama effect. (This will be covered more fully in the next chapter, but the cyclorama effect is achieved with a curving wall of green that goes from the wall of the greenscreen to the floor so that there are no hard edges for shadows to get caught in, which are very hard to key properly.) Manufacturers range from lower-budget companies like ImageWest and effects companies like Elsdon Enterprises FX (EEFX) to Rosco — the industry standard in gels, filters, and greenscreen backgrounds — with their DigiComp cloth. (The DigiComp line also extends to paint and tape, the latter of which can be used to connect cloth or foam screens and to create tracking marks for moving shots.)

Although you might be tempted to look for the least-expensive roll of greenscreen cloth you can find, it's important to keep the thickness of the cloth in mind. By and large, you want thick cloth because it can hold a deeper green color without getting washed out, is much less likely to wrinkle, and is also less likely to tear. Some companies make backdrops out of muslin, which, in my experience, is far too thin and wrinkly to do a decent job.

Rosco's material is fairly heavy-duty but doesn't have special backing, which means it's not completely wrinkle-free, but it does match perfectly with all the other products in Rosco's DigiComp color line, including tape and paint. A 5' x 30' bolt of cloth costs $110 to $120; a 5' x 60' bolt goes for $220 to $230. (If you're going to hang the cloth from a rod, you'll need to sew rod pockets into the cloth yourself.) DigiComp tape to cover seams or hold fabric in place will run you about $23 to $25 for a roll that's 2" wide by 165' long.

EEFX offers a special light-diffusing greenscreen fabric that's 1/4" thick, with a foam-core backing to prevent wrinkling and nylon backing behind that so it won't tear. Seamless rolls measuring 5' x 12' cost about $70 to $80, and EEFX will stitch together rolls all the way up to 20' x 30' for a medium cyclorama studio for less than $900. (They will also sew rod pockets to hang the fabric for an additional $15 to $50, depending on the size of the roll.)

Portable flexscreen

A portable flexscreen is probably the answer for most filmmakers who do not need full-length body shots. These screens pop open from a collapsed state, much like Photoflex reflector screens or those pop-out camping tents. While they can be a huge pain to re-collapse, overall they are extremely convenient. They can be stored almost anywhere; the material tends to be heavier than most cloth rolls; the frame stretches the fabric tight, so there are very few wrinkles; and most screens are green on one side and blue on the other, so that you can use one screen for both greenscreen and blue-screen work. Flexscreens can be bought for $60 to $400 from ImageWest, Lastolite, Photoflex, and Westcott.

A flexscreen can easily be assembled behind your talent and taken with you, whether in an ad hoc studio or in the field. Unfortunately, many flexscreens have a black border around them, which may cause compositing problems if you're not careful.

As useful as flexscreens are, many of them have an Achilles' heel: a black border. Why anyone would ever have created a greenscreen with a black border is beyond understanding, as any shots that show the entire screen must have the black frame rotoscoped out. Westcott appears to be the only manufacturer that makes a collapsible greenscreen with a green border. (Their 6' x 7' reversible screens with stand run about $300.)

The cutting edge: Chromatte

Chromatte is a special lighting/backing package manufactured by Reflecmedia that makes greenscreen compositing much easier. It consists of a heavy-duty fabric coated with tiny glass reflectors and an LED LiteRing

Chromatte uses a specially designed LiteRing that shines either blue or green light at a special reflective material.

that goes around the camera's lens. The Chromatte fabric — which comes in drapes for use in a studio or pop-out screens for location work — looks gray under normal lighting but is specially designed to reflect blue or green light emitted by the LiteRing, which includes a dimmer. You light your subject normally, then switch on the LiteRing and adjust it with the dimmer until the background glows with a perfectly even blue or green color, depending on which color of LiteRing you purchased. Because of the way the LiteRing is designed, it doesn't cast a tinted hue on your actors. And since special lighting doesn't have to be applied to the background screen, Chromatte setups require fewer lights and tend to key very cleanly.

There are some problems with this revolutionary form of chromakeying, though. First off, while the long-lasting LED LiteRings are reasonable at $600 per ring, the fabric itself is very pricey. At $32 a square foot, it'll run you $19,200 for a 30' x 20' drape for a midsize cyclorama. You can, however, get away with a smaller setup because you don't have to worry about spill nearly as much; a 7' x 7' drape with LiteRing goes for about $2,000.

Secondly, even though the LiteRing doesn't cast a hue on your actors, its highlight is reflected in certain types of wet or highly reflective surfaces. Avoiding reflective surfaces is something you tend to do in any form

Because the LiteRing (which attaches to the front of the camera) provides full illumination of the reflective background the Chromatte system uses, no separate lighting is required for the background.

of greenscreening, but it's impossible in extreme close-ups when the wet, reflective surface in question is the human eye. Rings of green or blue highlight show up in the irises of actors' eyes in these types of Chromatte shots, and you will have to either rotoscope them out via moving "red eye" (or, rather, "green eye") reduction or track the appropriate color behind the eyes themselves to make these shots usable. Your only other option is to very carefully choose your camera angle, zoom depth, and LiteRing dimmer levels to minimize or eliminate the likelihood of a highlight reflection showing up.

Nevertheless, when the price on this setup drops (or a competitor releases a lower-priced alternative), you should definitely consider adding it to your greenscreen arsenal because of the comparative simplicity of the lighting and the ease of keying.

CHAPTER 4: BUILDING YOUR OWN GREENSCREEN

Now let's consider some of the possibilities for building your own greenscreen. We've included both more permanent setups involving painted walls, cloth backdrops, and a full studio, and more portable options, like foam-core boards and the portable vinyl greenscreen.

We'll mainly focus on home-built and mixed options but will also cover purchasable components like paint, tape, and cyclorama fabric. There are often distinct advantages to going with professional supplies.

Creating greenscreens with rolled paper

Lots of art supply stores sell rolls of green paper ranging from 3' to 8' wide (typically for as little as $25 to $30 for a 4' x 200' roll). With a little work, you can build a stand that holds the paper on a spool so you can pull it down behind the actors, just as photographers do with rolled backdrops. You can easily pull down enough of the roll so that the actor can stand on the paper and be shot at full body length. If the roll is fairly narrow, be sure your talent's hands or body don't move past the edges of the greenscreen. Of course, if you're creating HD footage with an SD camera, you've already got this down to a science. (Shooting HD footage with an SD camera is fully described in Chapter 7.)

In addition to the traditional roll setup, you can tear off sheets of this paper and tape them to a wall with colored painter's tape or Rosco's DigiComp tape to create a larger greenscreen.

Painted greenscreens using walls, flats, and foam core

You'll typically use paint when you're working on something that's designed to be permanent, like the walls of a studio or a cyclorama. This isn't always the case, though. Paint can also serve for more temporary options, such as flats or foam core. Flats are usually large pieces of canvas built into rugged wooden frames and are great for creating a movable studio scenario that will allow you to put your greenscreens into more 3D layouts. Foam core is fairly cheap and light, so it can be used to create truly portable solutions. Unfortunately, it's also pretty easy to ding up, so you'll always want to have some paint handy on location for touchups.

You can buy professional chromakey paint, or you can make your own. Only a couple of manufacturers make greenscreen or bluescreen paint. EEFX makes some pretty good stuff, at about $50 a gallon, but a lot of professionals prefer Rosco, which sells for between $75 and $110 a gallon. Both manufacturers have made their paint match their fabric lines. According to the folks at Rosco, their paint is formulated to require only one coat, which means, in theory, that you should be able to cover twice

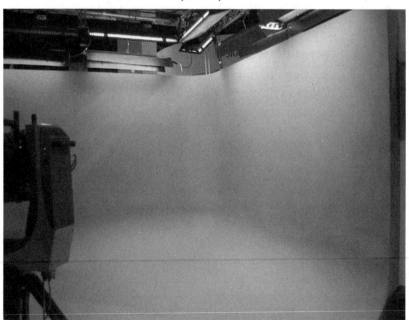

A cyclorama is a type of permanent greenscreen studio space that has a gentle curve between the wall and floor.

the surface area with it as with a gallon of the EEFX paint. EEFX states that you can cover 250 to 350 square feet per gallon, so we would presume the Rosco paint would double that. However, Rosco doesn't publish coverage statistics, so that can't be confirmed.

You can also make chromakey paint yourself. Tom Stern, one of our staff writers at *MicroFilmmaker* Magazine, went through the arduous process of calibrating his camera to color swatches he found at Lowe's and then painstakingly sampling each color in Photoshop to see which generated the most-pure green and the least gray. At the end of his testing, the mix he came up with that yielded the most-pure green was a matte-finish latex house paint made by Olympic/CCA called "Botanical Green." A gallon goes for about $10 to $15. Don't forget that you'll normally need two coats of paint to get a good, even finish.

Creating and hanging your own cloth backdrop

Rummage through your local cloth purveyors' stores and see if you can find cloth that's a true green, that's pretty heavy, and that's not too shiny. Take along a swatch of the Botanical Green mentioned above to test cloth colors against. You want to avoid fabrics with designs stitched into them and ones that are textured, like velvet. Once you've found a good fabric — probably a good high-thread-count broadcloth or muslin — get as much of it as you think you'll need. Remember that you'll probably be having your actors stand 6' to 10' away from the background cloth, so you'll need enough to stretch that far. Ask to have a spare fabric tube stapled to one end of the cloth; the heavy-duty cardboard roller will make a great spindle for your backdrop. If that's not possible, get a heavy-duty dowel rod that is about 2' to 3' longer than the width of your fabric. Be sure to either staple or nail one end of the fabric to the dowel or sew a rod pocket in the top of the fabric that the dowel can go through, so that the fabric can't come loose at the end.

Now you simply need to buy or construct some sort of backdrop support for the ends of the dowel or the tube. You can purchase backdrop support kits that are made from aluminum with an aluminum crossbar for $80 to $300. Or, more simply (and cheaply), you can affix loops of wire or rope to the ceiling or the top of the wall and slip the ends of the rod through the loops. For smoother rolling with a fabric tube, slip a dowel through the tube to create a rotating crossbar. For a more advanced setup, you can build a stand with dowels screwed into wide squares of wood at the base. Any form of U-shaped top piece can then serve to hold your dowel or roller. (With a little ingenuity, you can affix a pair of U-hook crossbar holders, which run between $10 and $20.) Use sandbags on the bases of homemade holders like this to keep the stand stable.

However you go about suspending your backdrop rod, you now have a background that can be rolled down and then rolled back up when you're done shooting.

The portable vinyl greenscreen

If you don't want to struggle with something as fragile as paper, don't want to try to keep foam from getting beaten up, and have found cloth too difficult to keep wrinkle-free, you can create a portable, roll-up greenscreen that's pretty durable, virtually wrinkle-free, and can be cleaned fairly easily.

We chatted with a few different greenscreen technicians and came up with a pretty simple how-to guide for building your own portable greenscreen for $60. This version is larger than most of the portable screens on the market (as well as being much easier to set up and collapse), and it creates a soft curve at the floor so you won't have any harsh shadows. (While professional chromakey paint can be used, we're listing the more economical homemade alternative in this walkthrough. Feel free to use whichever best fits your budget.)

Common household products can be employed to create a surprisingly sturdy vinyl greenscreen.

What you need to pull this off is some cheap vinyl flooring, which you can find at just about any home improvement store for about $40. Or see if your local flooring wholesaler needs to get rid of any horrendous-looking patterned vinyl flooring that isn't selling well. You'll be painting the back of the flooring, so it doesn't matter how obnoxious the front is, and you may be able to snatch up a really great deal.

The flooring needs to be heavy enough not to wrinkle or crease, and you'll need a uniform green color that is as close to what the camera perceives as pure green as possible and as opaque as possible.

Here's what you'll need and the approximate costs:

- 8' x 12' roll of vinyl flooring ($40)
- 1 gallon of matte latex house paint, mixed to the color Botanical Green ($11)
- 1 roller paintbrush ($5); I used an extendable one that made it much easier to do this project
- 1 paint pan ($2)
- A roll of large garbage bags ($2)
- A clean cardboard tube or piece of PVC pipe as thick and long as you can find (rummage for this item)
- Some packing or duct tape (you probably have some of this stuff floating around)

You will need to find a workspace large enough to allow you to lay out an 8' x 12' roll of vinyl in order to paint it. If you are in a dry environment, doing this outside will be fine. If you are in a location with high humidity or inclement weather, you'll need to find an indoor space.

1. Lay out trash bags as a spill guard below your roll of vinyl.
2. Unroll the vinyl so that the backing is face up.
3. Stir the gallon of paint and pour a decent amount into the paint pan.
4. Paint the backing evenly with one coat of paint. You'll probably want to do this in bare feet or booties to keep dirt off the screen as you work.
5. Let the paint dry for at least four hours before moving the green-screen. Ideally, you don't want to move the screen at all until the second coat has dried, but if that's not feasible, after four hours you can loosely roll the vinyl up, tape the top flap down, and let it dry standing up for another 16 to 20 hours or so.)

When painting, be sure to use clean bare feet or booties so as not to get dirt or creases on your vinyl siding.

6. Approximately 20 to 24 hours later, paint a second coat on the screen, being very careful to be as even as possible.

7. Allow the second coat to dry for another 20 to 24 hours.

8. After it is completely dry, wrap the greenscreen around a clean length of cardboard tubing or PVC pipe and tape the edge of the vinyl to the roll with packing or duct tape. Don't try cinching bungee cords around the roll (at least not for the first 14 days or so); you can cause the latex paint to adhere to the front side of the vinyl flooring. The first time I made one of these screens, I made the mistake of not using an internal roller and secured the roll closed with bungee cords. I ended up creating an unrollable, vinyl-green Tootsie Roll out of the whole thing!

Now you can take your new greenscreen wherever you need it. After it's completely dry, it's surprisingly rugged.

In order to rig a hanging version, you can fit reinforced grommets into the sides of the greenscreen and then attach it to rafters or other high-placed tie-down spots. Or you can use flooring staples to staple one edge of the screen to the cardboard roll or PVC pipe you rolled your screen around and hang it from a suspended rod slipped through the pipe. This will give you a window-shade greenscreen, which can be very useful.

Combining elements to create a cyclorama greenscreen studio

If you plan on doing a lot of intensive greenscreen work, building a cyclorama greenscreen studio is a really smart idea. A cyclorama is made with a greenscreen that curves from the wall to the floor so that there are no sharp corners or edges. This allows for more flexibility in your keys and cleaner keys, since sharp edges catch shadows in an unnatural way and show up as dark lines that are difficult to key properly.

There is a great deal of confusion about how much space you need for a greenscreen studio. You will want your actors to be at least 6' to 8' from your greenscreen wall, and then you will need your camera to be at least 6' to 8' feet from the actors for medium shots. For long shots, you will need to be as much as 12' to 22' from the subject, depending on the lens and the height of the actor. This means that, as a bare minimum, you need an area

3 wall seamless cyc with 16 feet to the grid. Credits: Director: Tiffany Dang, Company: Artemis Entertainment, Photo by: David Torno, Model: Hope Dang

with 20 square feet of usable space. Obviously, if you've been doing the math, it would be preferable to have an area that's 30 square feet or larger.

As you can imagine, folks who live in a single-room apartment are probably not going to be able to build a greenscreen studio at their residence. I've seen some innovators who have painted their apartments green and managed to get some fairly decent results, but that's very difficult. You really need to have a good-sized two-car garage, a large room in a Southern-style house, or some sort of rented studio or office space you can convert into a greenscreen studio. Or you can try contacting local colleges and universities, especially community colleges. With the growing popularity of greenscreen work, many colleges want to offer some sort of facility for this for their students and might be willing to let you construct a studio on their property in exchange for them being able to let their students use it. You can often work out a deal where some of the students will intern with your production company to help you build the studio, which is a great way to get free labor and might lead you to find someone worth working with in the future.

To create a cyclorama setup in your studio space, you could use cloth rolls, but this normally isn't the best option for a permanent studio for low-budget filmmakers. Most cloth can wrinkle fairly easily, gets dirty quickly, and is hard to join seamlessly with other pieces to make a backdrop. (I say "most" because the foam-backed cloth manufactured by EEFX avoids most of these problems and is fairly economical. It's more expensive than the method we're about to describe but a lot easier if you've got the funds for it.)

The better way to back a low-budget cyclorama is with five of the portable vinyl greenscreens described earlier. The great thing about this setup is that it's fairly inexpensive, yet it's resistant to wrinkling and as easy to clean as your wall. At full retail, you'll spend about $200 for five rolls of 8' x 12' flooring, which is enough to give you a 32'-wide panorama that's 8' high and has a cyc-curved floor that extends 3½' from the wall. In the central area, you'll have an extended floor 12' wide and 8' deep, for an effective long shot stage that extends 11' from the rear wall. (The following illustration shows the layout for a 24' cyclorama. The 32' one would include four panels on the wall instead of three.)

Affix a bar of a soft, sturdy wood like pine about 8' up on each of the walls you intend to use as greenscreen walls. Then, using screws about 1"

Basic Cyclorama

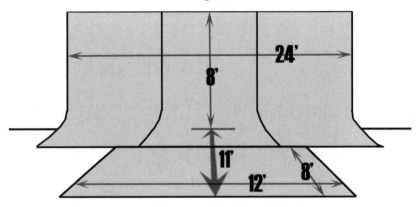

To expand this 24'-wide basic cyclorama to a 32' one, simply add one more vinyl greenscreen to the right or left side and slide the front stage in the appropriate direction until centered.

to 1½" longer than the wood bar's thickness, attach the edge of the vinyl flooring — with the painted side facing out — to the wall by driving the screws through the wood bar into the wall studs behind. Because the vinyl can tear, be careful not to screw through it at its very edge; leave an inch or two above the screws to be on the safe side. Now unroll the vinyl down the wall. It will naturally form a cyclorama curve at the bottom. Affix the vinyl to the floor with liquid nails, traditional nails, or screws, making sure to keep the cyclorama curve consistent. Proceed with each roll like this, making sure that the rolls' edges line up with one another. For the final touch, unroll the last roll and affix it to the floor in front of the bottom edges of the other rolls. This last roll forms your extended greenscreen stage.

If you would prefer to create a painted cyclorama stage, you will need to construct some sort of curved piece of wood, plastic, or plaster for where the wall and floor meet. Then you can paint your space with either home-made greenscreen paint or one of the professional paints such as those from Rosco and EEFX.

CHAPTER 5: GETTING YOUR BACKGROUND ENVIRONMENTS

Before we get to the section of the book that deals with production, we need to take a moment to discuss something absolutely essential to your greenscreen production: background environments.

While many filmmakers might be tempted to wait until after production to obtain backgrounds, this is not a good plan. Getting your background environments set up before production enables you to match lighting and camera angles precisely. If you have a live keyer like Adobe's Ultra CS3, you can even test-key camera shots on set to make sure they line up with the background image.

Below is a list of different ways to create or acquire background environments. You may already have thought of some of these sources, but others might jog your creativity in ways you hadn't expected. We've also noted things you should keep in mind about obtaining these environments.

Photography and videography

This is the most common place people turn to for backgrounds, figuring that they can either snap all the backgrounds they need or video them. You do need to consider a few things as you do so.

1. **Angle.** People taking pictures or shooting video with no one in the foreground tend to shoot from eye level at an angle that aims down toward the ground. But when people film talent in front of an actual background in a live action shoot, the camera is almost always lower — usually between chest and stomach level — and aimed straight

ahead or slightly up at the face of the actor. If you think about this before you shoot a background, you'll get much more realistic shots because you'll know to shoot from a lower angle.

2. **Image size.** Always shoot as large a size as you can. The bigger your image, the more you can do with it in post.

3. **Framing.** While it can be tempting to use your digital SLR or an HVX200A to get a background with some foliage framing the foreground, resist the urge! Foreground elements are a nightmare to rotoscope from a background. Always get clean background plates with no foreground elements. You can always add any foreground elements you want in post with much greater flexibility and power. We'll discuss this more a little later.

4. **Faces.** If you don't have permission to record someone's face, you can't use it in your film. While you could blur out the faces in post, this will always look hokey in anything that's not a documentary. So avoid shooting crowd backgrounds unless you've gotten all the participants to sign a mass waiver for you to use their faces.

5. **Trademarks.** Trademarks that are seen on buildings from the street are usually considered fair game for backgrounds, but trademarks in indoor settings are almost never legal for you to use. Make sure you avoid getting them into your backgrounds or you'll be trying to replace them with something realistic after the fact.

6. **Logical availability.** If you want to place everyone on a Hawaiian island and you live in Ohio, practically speaking you won't be able to acquire the background footage yourself. Consider stock footage instead; it's obviously going to be less expensive than a trip to Hawaii and likely will give you sizing options you might not be able to acquire yourself.

Digital matte paintings

Although matte paintings are not nearly as popular as they once were thanks to the advent of powerful 3D programs, the digital version of this technology is actually alive and well. If you have the skills to combine various elements in photographic, illustration, and painting programs to create photo-realistic backgrounds, then go ahead and do so! If you can't do this yourself, consider online artistic resources, like *www.renderosity.com*, which have many talented artists who might be willing to work with you.

3D models can be a great way to get realistic backgrounds, like this one created by Ralph Caldwell using Cinema 4D.

3D rendering

We'll discuss this in much more detail in Chapter 19, but 3D rendering is perhaps the ultimate way to create scenes you could never capture in the real world. It takes some time to learn a 3D program well enough to create photo-realistic environments, but there are many books on the subject and many video training options. Some companies, like Maxon (creator of Cinema 4D), have some extremely powerful training options, including both free and paid training. If you are interested in Cinema 4D tutorials, their Web site is *www.cineversity.com*. You can also find free tutorials at 3D sites like *www.daz3d.com* and *www.renderosity.com*.

Multilayered composites

This is one of the best ways to create backgrounds because it gives you a great ability to cheat the eye. A multilayered composite employs multiple types of elements in both the background *and* the foreground to really sell the idea of an immersive environment. Start with a clean photographic or videographic background plate. Try to obtain one that is larger than the size you need so you can pan across it or tilt down to achieve more of a sense of spaciousness. You can then add alpha channel elements, like a replacement sign, a different skyline, a particle physics fire, a rendered car, or a potted plant that was videographed in front of a bluescreen. Finally, you can combine all these in 3D space in After Effects or a similar 3D-powered compositing program so that you can move your "virtual" camera to get the most authentic-looking shots possible.

Public domain

Some older films, photos, and other assets are actually in the public domain because their copyright has lapsed or because the artist has chosen to make them available to the public. You'll have to research anything you use, but this can be a great way to put one of your actors in a 1920s or 1930s film for that vintage piece you've always wanted to do!

Internet and negotiation

With so many extremely talented photographers, videographers, matte painters, and 3D renderers showcasing their work on the Internet, it can be tempting to just rip off someone else's intellectual property. Even if you don't care about the ethics of doing this, keep the following in mind: The very fact that the Internet has made the world small enough for you to find out about a particular artist's work means it's likely small enough for them to find out that you used their work illegally! If they take legal action against you, you won't have a leg to stand on, and on top of all the other trouble you'll have caused yourself, you'll also find that your film can't be shown anywhere, ever!

Instead, contact these folks directly and see if they would be willing to let you use their work in exchange for credit in your film, deferred payment, or even your willingness to help them with a project down the road. You might be shocked at how many people want to contribute to something if it's creative and they can get some credit. Besides the fact that there's no danger of you getting sued, you might just make a friend in the process, and artists/photographers/renderers are often very willing to create or shoot custom backgrounds for you once they get involved. Just make sure you fill out a legal contract with them so that you've got everything in writing. Some film festivals won't accept your film and many distributors won't look twice at you if you don't have all your legal permissions in order.

Stock backgrounds

Using stock backgrounds can be surprisingly economical. Some Web sites have very beautiful and workable photographic backgrounds for as little as $5 to $50. For more complex options, you can often find video backgrounds for $50 to $200; some sites even have multilayered photographic or video-graphic backgrounds with separate layers and foreground objects for $60 to $300. Large companies like Artbeats and Shutterstock have a wide selection, but don't be afraid to surf the Internet for some of the other options available. A growing number of smaller production companies are making layered and video backgrounds for these purposes. For example, filmmaker (and *MicroFilmmaker* Magazine writer) Tom Stern is releasing a series of extremely high-resolution layered scenes of the ancient city of Jerusalem through his FILMdyne Productions company (see *FILMdyne.com*).

CHAPTER 6: LIGHTING YOUR MATTE FOR MAXIMUM KEYING SIMPLICITY

I f you're using the Chromatte system, you can skip this chapter. But if you're one of those for whom this isn't a viable option, keep reading.

The principles behind lighting your matte are best understood by looking at what you're trying to accomplish. Ideally, you are attempting to illuminate all parts of your background matte evenly so that the color is as uniform as possible. The fewer differences in color, the easier it is to pull a good key, and the fewer variations of the key you'll have to perform. In hard-to-key situations, you'll usually run several different versions of a key on multiple layers of the same subject, to try to get a combined key that is as clean as possible. Obviously, the more you have to do this, the harder it becomes and the more likely you are to remove detail or color from your main character.

The best illuminant for a matte is a cloudy day, which provides an even, soft light that's much closer to white than it is to blue. By contrast, unfiltered daylight, which runs between 5200K and 6500K color temperature, is very blue in appearance.

Custom-ordering cloudy days hasn't been figured out yet, and shooting outside is rarely a good idea anyway, so we've got to come up with a better way to light our mattes. The most common solution is soft boxes.

A soft box is a fixture that encases a light in a silver-lined fabric tent with a partially opaque front panel that diffuses light, causing it to be spread over a greater surface area. The greater the surface area and the closer the fixture is to an object, the softer the light. Soft light is light that is so omnipresent that it casts very few shadows; hard light, which comes from a single

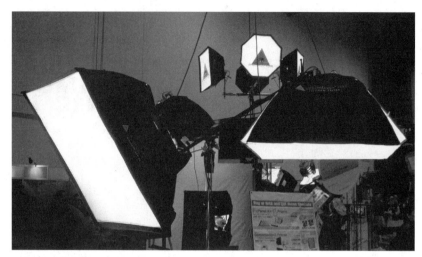

Soft boxes create soft, diffuse light that helps evenly light greenscreens and is flattering to people who are directly lit by them.

direction, casts very distinct shadows. If you move a soft box far enough away, the light it emits becomes hard because only very directional light beams reach your target.

Don't confuse the softness or hardness of a light with its power or intensity. Even if you move a soft box far enough away for it to effectively become a hard light, it will still have a weak illumination value because the diffusion on the soft box's front panel knocks down its intensity tremendously. In professional lighting rigs, you can vary the starting softness or hardness of a light via a dial that rotates between a soft floodlight and a hard spotlight, but the actual intensity is measured by the wattage that the light emits, such as 300W, 650W, or 1K.

You can get lighting rigs that are built into a soft box, or you can get soft boxes that can be placed over a pre-existing light rig. For one low-cost setup, Smith Victor makes a very nice incandescent/fluorescent soft box light called the KSB500, which costs about $200. Its included incandescent bulbs are 500W 3200K floods that cost between $3 and $5 and are rated to last about 200 hours, but the fixture can also take daylight-balanced fluorescent bulbs, like the recommended 55W 5200K Smith Victor FL55 bulb, which costs $46 per bulb and is rated to last about 6,000 to 8,000 hours.

With these lower-cost rigs, you obviously have less control and power, especially compared to a setup that's placed over a stand-alone lighting solution, like a Lowel or ARRI Fresnel. At *MicroFilmmaker* Magazine, we use an ARRI 300/650 Fresnel Combo Kit, which gives you four lights to work with and some nice controls, and makes lighting a good matte much easier. If you have a kit like this, you'll probably want to look into getting an add-on soft box, like the medium Photoflex CineDome Softbox, which is about 2' x 3' and runs about $210 at places like B&H Photo Video. When you add a soft box to a pre-existing professional light, you have the advantage of being able to add colored gels to your light before you put the soft box on it.

If that doesn't give you enough diffusion, you can buy professional diffusion frames that are much larger, or you can build your own with white nylon ripstop fabric fastened to a rectangular PVC pipe frame for under $30.

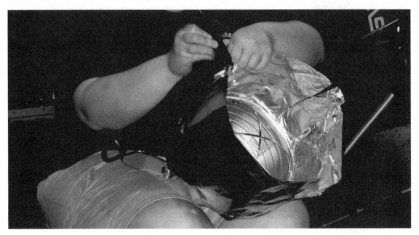

With careful cutting, aluminum foil can make ultra-low-budget barndoors on a clamp lamp.

If you really need to keep this inexpensive and can't afford the ARRI light kit or even the Smith Victor lights, are you out of luck? Not at all. You can still light your bluescreen or greenscreen with diffusion material and a little creativity. I've had fairly decent results using clamp lamps (the ones that are metal and have a porcelain fitting), which cost $10 to $15 at stores like Wal-Mart or Lowe's, and 500W 3200K GE photoflood bulbs, which go for $3 to $5 at various online retailers.

The difficult part of this sort of setup is that it can be hard to control the light, so you'll need to be creative with hanging your diffusion material to get as wide a spread of light as possible. Additionally, you may need to knock down some of the spread of the scoops using aluminum foil and heat-resistant tape to fashion makeshift barndoors.

Aluminum foil barndoors can have gels clipped to them just like professional barndoors, although greater care must be taken because they aren't as sturdy.

Whether you use a professional lighting solution or a makeshift one, preview the lighting of your greenscreen's background very carefully to make sure you have gotten things as evenly lit as possible and that the light is as close to 50 IRE as possible.

A professional light meter will enable you to test for consistency very accurately. If you can't afford a light meter, you can still test for consistency with a few creative work-arounds. If the options for your camera's "zebra" (a diagonally striped graphic display that shows when things are lit at a preselected brightness) allow you to set it as low as 50 to 60 IRE, you can use it to test lighting consistency. (Panasonic cameras don't allow this low a setting, but others may.)

If your camera does not go this low, you can use video monitoring software packages like Adobe's OnLocation (PC) or Divergent Media's ScopeBox (Mac) for testing. Set either to 50 IRE and try to make sure you're getting a consistent reading across the entire matte. To check for hotspots, flip your zebra setting to 60 and see if you're still getting the zebra

Adobe OnLocation is one of the more popular video caption and light/color monitoring software packages available for both PCs and Macs.

stripes. If they're still there at 60, you need to decrease your light's intensity with diffusion or by using different wattage bulbs to get consistent, even light on your background close to 50 IRE.

Positioning your lights effectively

To understand the optimal distance for lighting, you must understand the inverse square law. The inverse square law as applied to illumination states that the strength of a light on an object varies in inverse proportion to the square of the distance from the source of the light. In other words, light doesn't drop off at a constant rate the way you might think it would as it gets farther from its source, but at a rate equivalent to the square of the distance it has traveled.

Actual numbers make this a little easier to understand. You would think that if you moved a light illuminating an object from 4' away to 8' away, you would be getting 50% of the original light on the object; by doubling the distance, you'd be halving the light. In reality, though, you only get 25% of the original light; doubling the distance gives you a quarter as much light — the reduction equals the square of the distance. If you were to move the light four times as far away, you would be getting 1/16

Lighting Inverse Square Law

$$I = K/D^2$$

I = Intensity
K = Light Output
D = Distance

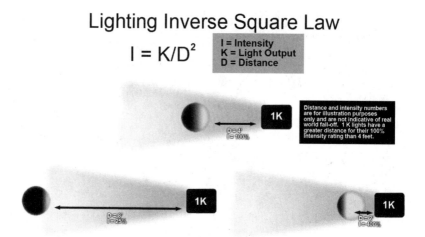

The inverse square law states that if you double the distance between your light and your subject, your light output is reduced to one quarter. However, if you halve the distance, your light output quadruples.

as much light, again squaring the distance. Conversely, if you were to move your light from 4' to only 2', you'd quadruple the power of the light as you halved the distance.

What are the implications for greenscreen illumination? If you have the room to move your lights nearer to or farther from your screen, you can make radical illumination changes in a small amount of space. If you don't have the room to move your lights in order to make adjustments, then you need to make changes either by using more powerful or less powerful lights, or by increasing or decreasing the number of lights.

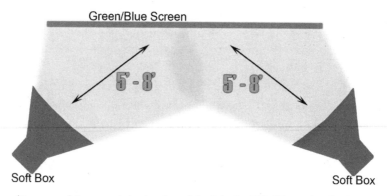

By angling your soft boxes precisely, the edges of the light (or "falloff") cancel each other out so that there is a uniform wash of light across the greenscreen.

While each lighting setup is different, you usually want to have your lights between 5' and 8' away from your screen. Again, to make sure you're getting even lighting, test your illumination range with the zebra either in your camera or in your waveform monitor in an OnLocation or ScopeBox laptop, trying to keep the illumination as close to 50 IRE as possible.

Types **of lighting**

You can choose from a number of different lighting types. The following are some of the more popular options for lighting greenscreens and bluescreens.

Incandescent lights — 3200K in color temperature — have a warmer tone and generate more heat than other types. They're good for lighting smaller greenscreens in setups with soft boxes or other diffusion, but their heat and lower life span can be problematic for long shoots. Pricing can run from $15 for an extremely makeshift setup to many thousands of dollars for professional lighting rigs.

Fluorescent lights are cool-running lights that tend to have a greenish hue if they are not properly color-balanced. Fluorescents can be positioned in vertical banks on either side of a greenscreen or cyclorama and produce fairly even lighting — their falloffs cancel each other out. Be

The ARRI 300-650 Fresnel kit is a basic professional kit that creates light in the incandescent, 3200K range.

aware, though, that standard fluorescent banks from home improvement stores have a tendency to flicker, which changes the illumination on your background in an unacceptable way. You need ones equipped with specially designed flicker-free ballasts. Companies like Studio Lighting Systems sell basic two-tube banks for $350 and four-tube banks for $800 to $900. More robust systems like those from industry standard Kino-Flo tend to start at $800 for a two-tube bank and go up.

Cyc lights are quartz lights set in a curved reflective backing and are designed to be mounted in a curved, horizontal group above and below a greenscreen. Each bulb's falloff combines with its neighbor's to create an evenly lit surface. They're very useful for both larger greenscreen and cyclorama studio setups, but be aware that they can also create overly bright areas that can raise your greenscreen's IRE, so take care when using them. Made by specialty lighting companies like Altman, cyc lights start at $200 to $300 for a single light and can go for much more. An array of four lights will cost you $600 for a horizontal, floor-based setup and up to $1,000 for a hanging cluster for overhead illumination.

LED lights are very bright, very cool lights that often can be adjusted to different color temperatures. One LED light manufacturer, Zylight,

Zylight is just one manufacturer of the increasingly popular LED light fixtures, which have extremely long life spans.

makes a version that can also adjust its native tint without gels to any color you desire, a great attribute for greenscreen work. They have extremely long life spans — 100,000 hours or more — and range in price from $150 to $1,500, depending on power, evenness of light, and other considerations.

Additional lighting elements to make your colors "pop"

The most important thing to remember when it comes to making colored backgrounds pop is that, in addition to getting diffuse light, you want to try to get nonwhite light. Why? White light is less likely to make a greenscreen glow than green light. The same holds for bluescreens with blue-tinted light.

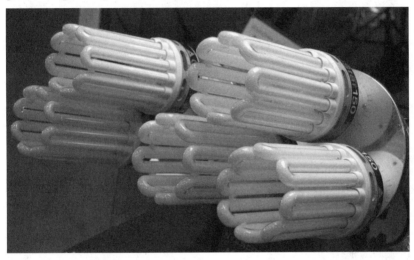

Screw-in fluorescent bulbs can be used in semiprofessional fixtures and clamp lamps and can be purchased at the high Kelvin spectrum that will cause a bluescreen to "pop."

This is the one area where bluescreens have a huge advantage. Light temperature is measured on the Kelvin scale, which relates temperature to the color that metal (such as the metal filaments still prevalent in most bulbs) turns as it gets hotter. The hotter metal gets, the more blue the glow becomes. The Kelvin temperature scale starts with a very orange color and gets more and more blue as temperature increases. The standard for most indoor lighting is 3200K, which is fairly orange in color temperature. Standard replication of daylight rises to 5600K, which falls into the blue region of the color temperature scale. To get even bluer lighting, I have found screw-in fluorescent bulbs online rated at 6500K, running about $20 or so. That's a great deal, with about twice the power of the FL55 bulbs mentioned earlier at less than half the cost. Using the bluest, flicker-free light you can find will give you a very vibrant bluescreen. Just make sure it is properly diffused, and if it's not flicker-free, the vibrancy of your background will shift too much. (You can also combine such Kelvin "loading" with some of the options we mention in the following greenscreen section.)

It's not as easy to light greenscreens and make the color glow, but it is by no means impossible. There are three pretty simple approaches, two of which are more expensive and the third very inexpensive — but somewhat trickier.

Gel manufacturers like Rosco offer a variety of different types of gels for all sorts of lighting needs, including boosting chromakey colors or creating the correct tint for your key lighting.

First is perhaps the oldest method: adding gels to your lights. This works well for ARRI, Lowel, and other lights that have barndoors; gels can be purchased from manufacturers like Rosco, Lee, and Apollo and tend to run about $6 to $7 per 20" x 24" sheet. You can also get them in sampler packs to experiment with for between $30 and $80. With very powerful gels you should be able to cast colored light without diffusion, but you're most likely to have better results if you clip a soft box, like the Chimera or PhotoFlex Cinedome soft boxes, over your professional light. A 24" x 32" PhotoFlex Cinedome soft box costs a little over $200.

If you are using fluorescents instead of traditional incandescent lights, you can get tube-style gels that are designed to slide over the fluorescent tubes. Most tube gels run about $12 to $20 apiece. Also keep in mind that fluorescent lights that haven't been specially colored often have a somewhat greenish hue to them, which can make your coloring job easier.

If you are using an all-in-one soft box solution, you can also get large pieces of gel and affix them to the corners of the soft box. Gel rolls can usually be picked up for about $100 for a roll 24" x 25' or $160 for a roll 48" x 25'.

The only cautionary note with the gel method is that the stronger the coloration of your gel, the more it will subdue your light's output. For example, if you use 1/2 green on your light, you'll lose 1/2 f-stop's worth of light, but if you go up to 3 or 4 green, you're losing 3 or 4 f-stops' worth of light.

Because of light loss with gels, a lot of people have started turning to LED lights, which can create bright, colored light without gels. Some manufacturers offer only limited color-shift options, but Zylight has created some small, powerful lights that give you a full range of outputs. Currently available are the more omnidirectional Z50 and the slightly more focused Z90, both of which consist of multiple LED lights in a cube format. The Z50 model combines more than 230 elements into a square inch and uses only 30 watts of power, producing more than 160° of soft light with no hotspots. The Z90 model renders more than 130° of output. Each Zylight is rated for 50,000 hours of usage before factory recalibration is needed. Multiple Zylights can be networked by remote to create a larger unit.

Creating light at the frequency you want with something like the Zylight means you aren't wasting power as you do when you must gel

Zylights can be networked together in a lighting array for permanent studios. While their price tag is a bit hefty currently, when that drops, they might be an excellent choice for many low-budget filmmakers.

down a more powerful light. LEDs also run incredibly cool. Both these factors make LEDs a great solution for small, portable greenscreen setups, but they quickly get expensive if you're lighting an entire greenscreen studio with networked Zylights. The Z50 runs between $700 and $750 per light, the Z90 between $900 and $950 — figures that really add up in a networked arrangement.

The final option is potentially the most inexpensive, but you need to be very careful to make sure that you don't start a fire. Semitranslucent ripstop nylon fabric in green can work as diffusion for your lights. (A 36" x 60" swatch of 1.9 oz. ripstop nylon costs about $7 or $8.) The green fabric will essentially work as both a diffusion and a gel, so you can save yourself the cost of gels by creating diffusion flats with it. Simply construct a stable framework out of PVC pipes and then affix your fabric to the front using wires or even sturdy thread. Place your lights behind the screen, and light away! Just don't let the fabric get too near hot lights.

With all of these options, don't neglect to check the zebra in your camera or the vectorscope in your laptop so you don't go overboard and make the background *too* bright. Remember, you're shooting for 50 to 55 IRE in brightness for the background.

CHAPTER 7: LIGHTING AND POSITIONING YOUR TALENT FOR OPTIMAL BLENDING

Preplanning the lighting to blend between foreground and background planes

One of the biggest challenges in keying is matching the lighting from the foreground plate (the footage of your actor that you've shot in front of a greenscreen) with the background plate (the artificial environment you wish to put your actor into in post). There are a whole host of theories about simplifying things, from writing down all the lighting conditions when you acquire background footage or images to using translucent items (like balloons) when recording a test plate, as these objects permit limited light transference for measuring lighting strength, direction, and color. Of course, it's always good to use a swatch with three luminance (brightness) shades on it — black, medium gray, and white — when acquiring your background plates and in the first few seconds of your foreground plate. It will be much easier to match colors in post if you do so.

But what about when you want to place your actors in a galaxy far, far away or in a fantasy kingdom that doesn't really exist? For these situations, you can render the backgrounds yourself with a program like NewTek Lightwave (*Sin City* and *The 300*), which works really well for 3D backgrounds; or for fantasy you could use a program specifically for nature backgrounds like e-on Vue 6 Infinite (*Pirates of the Caribbean: Dead Man's Chest* and *The Spiderwick*

Chronicles). In both cases, you'll likely have access to information about the lighting that you can use to match plates. If you're not very comfortable with rendering or don't have a good 3D setup, you'll be using stock footage — and facing the problem of not knowing precisely how it was lit.

My recommendation for matching your lighting when using stock footage is simply to look at the background footage and make notes about the lighting. Is the scene outdoors or indoors? If it's outdoors, is it direct sunlight or a cloudy day? If it's direct sunlight, about where in the sky does the light appear to be coming from and what hue does the sunlight appear to be? Sunlight changes hue throughout the day, with a less-blue cast of 5000K at dawn, increasing to 6500K at noon, then going back down to a lower Kelvin range by sunset. If the scene is indoors, do there appear to be multiple lighting types intermingling, such as artificial lighting and sunlight coming through a window? Noting all these sorts of things will really help you match your foreground and background lighting.

Now we need to discuss the types of lighting you can choose for your foreground.

Different types of lighting for your foreground

Directional lighting can be used to match many types of situations, from indoors to outdoors, but is most appropriate in outdoor, sunny locations. Directional lighting includes, of course, a powerful light source, called a key light, that illuminates the actor, and a less powerful light, called a fill light, to fill in areas of the face or body not directly illuminated by the key light.

Side lighting can be a very stark way to light your subject, which is often well suited to noir thrillers or sci-fi epics. It's especially beneficial for greenscreen because side lighting doesn't cast extra illumination on the background.

The combination prevents the subject from being too starkly lit. (Some directors will, however, intentionally use very weak fill lights to create a stark, "noir" look.)

The most common form of directional lighting is called triangle lighting. Imagine the setup as if the subject were at the center of a clock. The key light should be at 4:30, a fill light at 7:30, and a low-strength backlight, often called a kicker, positioned at 11:00, to help separate the subject from the background. Kickers are especially useful in greenscreen productions because they can be equipped with a colored gel to further separate the actor from the greenscreen.

Another popular form of directional lighting is sidelighting, in which one side of an actor's face is brightly lit by a powerful key light exactly perpendicular to the actor's line of sight on one side, with the fill light on the opposite side. This is a very thematic style of lighting that can be quite attractive. You can include a kicker behind the actor's head, but you need to be careful that it's not too powerful because kickers are more noticeable in sidelighting setups.

Flat lighting is low-contrast lighting that provides little or no shadowing, but is normally of a greater intensity than diffuse lighting. This isn't terribly common, especially since there are a limited number of backgrounds in which it wouldn't look artificial. You will, however, find flat lighting being used for indoor settings like hospitals and office buildings.

Diffuse lighting is more common than flat lighting because it tends to make the talent look more attractive. It works best when the background is a very cloudy day or a well-lit living room with powerful sconces bounced off the ceiling. Here's another important consideration: Because diffuse lighting covers up far more blemishes than directional lighting and thus can enhance the attractiveness of a female face, many lighting directors always light women with soft, diffuse lights regardless of the scenario. As a result, in greenscreen work you can get away with lighting women with soft boxes even in environments for which it might not seem entirely appropriate.

For more information on lighting your talent well, there's a great, economical training package from lighting trainer Bill Holshevnikoff called *The Power of Lighting for Film & Video.*

Placement of the actor and other blocking considerations

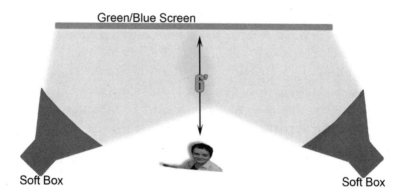

Placing the actor no closer that 6' from the greenscreen will help minimize any possibility of spill.

Actors placed improperly in front of a greenscreen can get reflected color, called spill, on them. You can mute your greenscreen's illumination a bit to prevent this, but it's usually better to simply move your actors farther from the screen. How far away should this be? To be on the safe side, a distance of 6' to 8' is best — and if you're using an actual bluescreen, be aware that blue tends to spill a lot farther than green.

Besides distance, you also need to think through what camera shots you're going to be getting in order to determine the actual placement of the actors. Try to schedule all wide, full-body shots on a single day so you can have those scenes done together, especially if you only have a temporary cyclorama. Most other typical film shots (close-ups, medium close-ups, and extreme close-ups) can be knocked out with a collapsible greenscreen or rolled-paper background.

Tricks to popping your talent from the background

One of the oldest tricks in the book for popping your talent out from the background is to add a color gel to the backlight that is the opposite color of your screen. For greenscreens, this would be magenta, for bluescreens, straw or yellow. Doing so will kill any spill during production so you don't have to mess with it in post — using postproduction spill killers can damage some of the other colors in your scene.

Adding a subtle gel to the backlight can help pop your subject from the keying background.

Although this is a good technique, you need to be subtle with it. If you go overboard at all, you can end up with bizarre edge tinting that looks just as artificial as the spill you're trying to avoid. We recommend nothing stronger than 1/4 to 1/2 f-stop gels.

Try a scene with the colored backlight and then one without as an experiment. Some keying programs have extremely good color spill algorithms that do very little damage to the other colors in your scene, so you may find that you don't need to use the colored backlighting to get good clean keys with little or no spill damage.

CHAPTER 8: CAMERA TECHNIQUES FOR CLEAN KEYS

Every camera is different. In this section, though, we'll try to give you some general ideas about how to place any camera, whether you should try to move it, what the best color settings might be, and a number of other issues relating to cameras and keying.

Optimal distance and behavior of your camera

It's best to have your camera about the same distance from your talent as the talent is from the background — between 6' and 8' away — for optimal separation between subject and background. Use a zoom to cut the distance if necessary.

I generally recommend locked-down shots because, quite frankly, they are easier to key. Additionally, some movements, like tilting up or down, can be performed pretty effectively in post with locked-down shots.

If you really want to do a dolly shot, you'll need to put tracking marks on your background. These are normally small dots or Xs made of tape that are applied at regular intervals to the greenscreen. They allow the camera movement across the greenscreen to be reliably tracked in post via trackers such as the one in After Effects, or more specialized plug-ins like the economical Imagineer Systems mocha-AE. (The larger Mocha software package was used by the creative minds behind the movie *Dirty Trousers* for their tracking needs.) Then you can link — or "slave" — your replacement background to the tracking data and have it move at the same speed as your camera. You can use a garbage matte to delete the tracking marks from your composition. If you're using dark tape for tracking, make sure that your subject never passes between these marks and the camera, or you will have to remove the dots

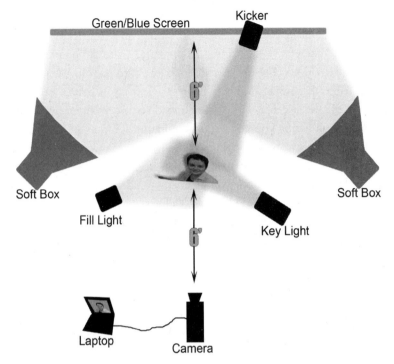

This gives you a feel for the placement of the background, the background lights, the actor, the foreground lights, the kicker, and the camera.

frame by frame in post, a tedious process called rotoscoping. If your tracking marks *must* pass behind your subject, make them out of tape that is a slightly lighter green than the screen so that they can still be tracked but can be keyed out with a second pass in your keyer. (For more on rotoscoping and removing tracking dots, turn to page 114.)

Setting up your camera for great keys

Optimal settings for cameras are a difficult thing to talk about, because every camera is different. Also, some issues are hotly disputed, like whether it's necessary to shift the way your camera reads coloration.

There is a long-standing argument between different greenscreen shooters about camera settings and coloration. Some swear by custom-tweaking their cameras to record green (or blue) with greater saturation, contending that this yields cleaner keys. Other shooters claim that adjusting the saturation can lead to problems recording other colors, and that correct illumination of the screen and modern keying software make special color settings on cameras unnecessary. I use Panasonic cameras and — after talking with *MicroFilmmaker* Magazine's technical writer Tom Stern when I first got into greenscreen — I set mine to the Cine Gamma D and CineColor settings. I've had good results, with good clean keys and no negative effects on my subject's coloration. For whatever camera you have, I recommend shooting different scenes with different settings and seeing which keys the best while still giving you good tonal coloration for your subject.

Beyond the question of color settings, we get into areas that are largely undisputed. First, if your camera shoots progressive images, be sure to choose this setting, because it will give you a cohesive field of color to key. Interlaced footage is recorded in two fields that intersect like needles on offset combs; if you try to key off such partially out-of-sync images, you'll have trouble getting clean keys. If your camera doesn't record true progressive, you'll need to invest in a true progressive converter, like Red Giant Magic Bullet Frames, which retails for $200 and converts interlaced footage to progressive.

Second, if your camera can handle it, shoot 24fps as opposed to the 30fps that's normal for video. The slower frame rate — the same as for film — will record more light. Just make sure that you prevent motion blur by setting your actual shutter speed to 1/48 or 1/96 of a second. (If your project needs to be 30fps, you can prevent motion blur with 1/60 or 1/120 of a second shutter speed.)

Third, turn off in-camera sharpening. It's an artificial way for the camera to try to make hard edges around objects being shot, and its interpretations often look fake and unnatural when it comes time to key things. Just turn it off.

Fourth, if you can record at a higher resolution than you will ultimately need, do so. This is especially useful if you have an HDV or HD camera but will be creating SD movies. If you shoot higher resolution footage, you can key at a higher resolution and then decrease the size of the keyed footage afterward. Your edges will be much cleaner, because any flaws in your key will be minimized substantially when you downsize.

Fifth, white-balance your camera with the lights illuminating the greenscreen turned *off*. Why? The amount of colored illumination reflected off the screen tends to interfere with the camera's interpretation of what white truly is. So it's best to turn off the screen's lights and white-balance using only the lighting for your subject. If you're using gels, white-balance with the gels removed from your subject lights. When you put the gels back on, you'll get a much more dramatic color shift from them.

Sixth, do not use a 35mm lens adapter on your camera when you are shooting greenscreen footage. Although I love the shallow depth of field you can get from a 35mm lens adapter like the Redrock Micro M2 or the LetusDirect LetUs35, it is absolutely what you do *not* want when you are shooting greenscreen. The goal is to get clean edges that are in focus; a 35mm lens adapter is designed to create soft edges by using shallow depth of field. Don't worry, though. If you want creative control of depth of field, all the shallow depth of field effects and rack focuses you could ever want can be applied in post — so long as you've gotten a good, clean key to work with.

Finally, once you have the camera set up, record a few seconds of the lit greenscreen before your actors step in front of it. Some greenscreen software packages, like Adobe Ultra, make use of such clean greenscreen plates to get a more precise key.

Creating **High-Definition footage with a Standard-Definition camera**

What happens if you want to create a High-Definition movie but have an SD camera like the DVX100? Believe it or not, you're not out of luck. With a little creativity you can bend your camera's resolution to serve your needs. The highest-resolution footage commonly used in HD cameras is 1080 pixels x 720 pixels. An SD camera, like the DVX100, shoots 720 pixels x 480 pixels. Simply turn your camera on its side (at a 90° angle) and you can record greenscreen footage at the 720-pixel high standard of HD. Obviously, this isn't quite as handy as having an HD camera. For one thing, your actors have a lot less room for gesturing and arm movement since they only have 480 pixels of side-to-side room, rather than 1080. But when you're done filming, you can import the footage into your favorite editor, flip the footage 90°, and key it into your HD film. With a little more creativity and skill, you'll be able to shoot many single actors and composite them in separate layers to give the composite depth and to make it seem like they were all on stage at the same time.

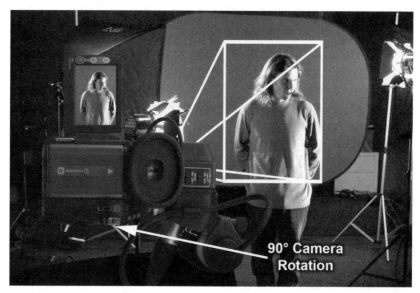

Want to shoot an HD film, but don't have an HD camera? With a little creativity, you can shoot sideways and get HD resolution.

CHAPTER 9: PRODUCTION IDEAS FOR CREATIVE GREENSCREEN USES

When I looked at writing a book about keying and compositing, I thought about the myriad possible uses I could discuss — a virtually endless list. Some are so innovative that I could have wrapped individual chapters around them. Some of them might not be quite so pivotal, but they're worthy of inclusion because they could very well spur creativity.

This next section is for those in the second camp. Hopefully the examples here will inspire you to try new things in the world of compositing.

The invisible man

This technique has been used to create everything from invisible people to the Ghost Rider. You use chromakey blue or green fabric to make a full bodysuit for your actor, including full-length gloves and a mask over the face. If you use blue fabric and shoot in front of a bluescreen, everything will vanish but any clothes worn over the bodysuit. If you're creative, you might pull off a dual-layer screen by using a greenscreen and a blue bodysuit. This enables you to greenscreen out the background and then bluescreen out the actor or actors. It's a great technique if you want to replace a person's face or body with a 3D model. (You need to put tracking dots on your actor's bodysuits and use a special mocap software package for this effect, which is a much more advanced technique than we'll cover in this book.)

Perhaps one of the more creative variations I've seen of this technique was used by David Torno and the folks at SydeFX Ink for the Flight of the Conchords' "Ladies of the World" music video. In the video, the Conchords' two singers have to roller-skate professionally while singing, which was something they could not do. SydeFX shot footage of two stunt doubles with similar hairstyles skating instead, then wrapped the singers with greenscreen fabric and recorded them singing in front of a greenscreen. When the green was keyed out, they had singing heads that could be motion tracked over the heads of the stunt doubles in After Effects. The final render is completely convincing.

Sin City makeup

For extreme Day-Glo effects like the bandages or the brilliant lipstick in *Sin City*, have your main actress wear bright green lipstick and key in a more brilliant color in post; for bandages, use green tape, like Rosco's DigiComp tape, then key them with a much brighter color of fabric in post. (For more information, turn to page 127.)

Luma keying

Luma (or brightness) keying is a way to screen a background not with color, but with brightness. Most commonly, it involves using a pure black or pure white background. Luma keying can be a great way to work around the color limitations of DV/HDV/HD cameras (remember that more luminance data than color data is recorded by most of these cameras). However, it usually doesn't work out for most low-budget filmmakers because, quite frankly, when you're trying to key by light levels, you have to have your lighting amazingly precise to create a pure white or pure black background. If it's not that precise, a white background will backlight your subject far too much, and a black background can blend with shadows on your subject. As we've suggested elsewhere, it's not a bad idea to try out this technique if you're dealing with a situation where you think you can have enough control over your luminance.

Shooting flame or smoke

Many low-budget filmmakers are content to purchase pre-keyed flame or smoke elements pre-composited from *VideoCopilot.net* or to create them dynamically in Particle Illusion. But if you want to create a realistic fire or a smoke cloud "by hand," make sure you shoot it in front of either a black or a white background; a colored background would tint such translucent items. Michele will show you how to use layer modes instead of keying to extract the effect starting on page 128.

Stop-motion animation

This may be hard to believe, but some of the highest-resolution, easiest-to-key footage you can get your hands on can be had with a camera that costs less than $500. That's because a digital SLR like the Nikon D40, which runs about $499, is capable of recording a 6.1MP image — double the resolution of 1080p HD — with the full spectrum of color. Most digital cameras are able to shoot in burst mode, which isn't fast enough for actual video but at 2 to 5 frames per second is plenty fast enough for stop-motion work.

So a digital SLR is a great way to go if you want to create HD stop-motion animation. For keying the pictures, try a stand-alone program like FXHome's PhotoKey or get a greenscreen plug-in that will work with Photoshop, like Digital Film Tools zMatte. You can then import all of your stills into any image program that has the ability to combine still images into animation, like Adobe Photoshop CS3 (or above), and then export them out as a movie. You could, of course, also create the movie from your unkeyed footage, but you will actually get a better key if you key the still images at their original size and then decrease the size of the images to HD afterward; you'll also be able to dolly or pan across your composited subjects in post, which can be very useful.

CHAPTER 10: PRODUCTION RULES TO SHOOT BY

An example of a low-budget shoot with the AG-HVX200A. Reprinted with permission from Vanderpool Films and Panasonic.

Before we move on to Michele's chapters on the postproduction side of things, I've summarized most of the key points made so far in the following list of production rules.

16 rules to shoot by

1. **Make sure that your background is opaque and without wrinkles.** This applies whether you have a permanent, enclosed greenscreen studio or a temporary setup. Thick fabric, linoleum, pop-out screens, foam core, and painted walls can all be fully serviceable backgrounds if they meet these criteria.

2. **Keep at least 6' between the actor and the greenscreen and 6' between the camera and the actor.** This prevents shadows from hitting the background and lowers the amount of "spill" — reflected green that can wash over your subject.

3. **Use soft boxes or some sort of diffuse light to light your greenscreen.** While a set of ARRI lights with Photoflex soft boxes or a bank of fluorescent lights will get you really nice results,

we've also had good outcomes using the twin 500W Smith Victor Economy soft boxes of their KSB1000. With a little creativity and some heatproof diffusion, you can also use three 500W 3200K flood bulbs in clamp scoops (the ones that have porcelain fittings and that are widely available at home improvement stores) for about $40 total. You'll need to pay really close attention to Rule No. 6 if you do this, though.

4. **Try a contrasting gel clipped to your kicker light to eliminate spill.** This is an old technique that's effective if you don't go overboard on the intensity of the gels you use. Going overboard will give you weird spill across the head and shoulders of your subject, in the opposite color spectrum from what would normally be expected, which is harder for a keyer to get rid of. For bluescreens a constrasting gel would be 1/2 straw or 1/2 yellow; for greenscreens, it would be 1/2 magenta.

5. **Use colored bulbs or colored gels to make your greenscreen more vibrant and, therefore, easier to key.** Beware of overlighting your background, but if you can add more of the background's color to its lighting, you'll get richer color. For bluescreens, you can use soft boxes equipped with non-flickering fluorescent bulbs that are between 5000K and 6500K (for $20 to $45). For greenscreens, try a color-calibrated green gel like Rosco's DigiComp gels. You can get them in sheets for clamping to barndoors and scoops, or in tubelike cylinders that fit around traditional fluorescent bulbs. Just remember that the stronger the color of your gels, the more they decrease the amount of light that actually passes through.

6. **Use the zebra settings in your camera or a light meter to test that you have even lighting across the background.** Using a light meter or your zebra settings makes it easier to check that you have no more than a 10% variance in illumination in any part of the greenscreen that will be filmed. You can use a traditional handheld light meter, but my recommendation is that you plug your camera into a laptop with some sort of light meter software in it. Adobe's OnLocation (which was Serious Magic's DVRack) is an excellent example for the PC, as is Divergent Media's ScopeBox for Mac. If you have a software package like Adobe Ultra, you can actually do test keys to see how well you've lit things and how likely you are to get a good

key. If you don't have a light meter or a laptop with the necessary software, you can turn your camera into a light meter by adjusting the two zebra levels on your camcorder and zooming in on different parts of your screen with the auto-iris turned on. If you adjust the zebra levels close enough to each other, you'll be able to make sure that you're within a 10% illumination variance throughout your screen.

7. **Don't overlight your greenscreen.** You want the background to be as close to pure green as possible. If you overlight the background, you'll wash out the green color and have difficulty keying the background properly. There's also a greater chance that green light will spill on your subject. Try to keep your illumination around 50 IRE.

8. **Light your main actors dynamically and with separate lighting from your greenscreen illumination.** The lighting should look like that in the background you will be adding in post, and will often be three-point light — consisting of a key light, a fill light, and a kicker. The most realistic keys match this perfectly. Make sure that you spread your key and fill lights a bit wider than normal to prevent their light from getting on the greenscreen, which could cause you to run afoul of Rules No. 6 and 7.

9. **Turn off all the lights illuminating the greenscreen before white-balancing.** If you white-balance with the greenscreen illuminated, you won't get a good white balance, which can cause the green to become washed out. Just don't forget to turn the greenscreen lighting on before you shoot your sequences!

10. **Experiment with your camera until you get the settings that yield the most difference between your actor and the colored background.** Each camera is different, but the more true green your camera can record for the background, the easier your shooting will be to key. For the extremely popular DVX100 and HVX200A, *MicroFilmmaker* Magazine's technical writer Tom Stern has determined through a number of technical tests that the best options are the Cine Gamma D setting combined with the CineColor setting. As mentioned earlier, there's some dispute about adjusting your camera settings. Some filmmakers feel it can negatively affect the coloration of your main character. While I haven't personally run into this with my own Panasonic cameras, be sure to do some extra experimentation with your own camera.

11. **Set your camera to get the fewest artifacts and least blur by turning off in-camera sharpening, shooting with high shutter speed (like 1/60 for 30fps, 1/50 for 25fps, or 1/48 for 24fps), and keeping your foreground subject in focus.** In-camera sharpening in video cameras makes keeping foreground objects in focus much easier. However, it creates artifacts and an artificial edge around your subject that looks fake when you key it. Although you don't want an artificial edge, you do want as clean an edge as possible, which is where shutter speed and focus come into play. The faster your shutter speed, the less motion blur you introduce, and therefore the cleaner your edges are. As motion blur is very difficult to key out but very easy to add in post, you want to avoid recording it as much as possible. Sharp focus of your subject is an additional way to make sure you have clean edges that you can key correctly.

12. **Shoot progressive footage if you have the option.** If your camera is capable of shooting progressive footage, use it instead of interlacing, which makes clean keys harder and would have to be removed in post anyway. If you must shoot interlaced, Red Giant Magic Bullet Frames, which costs about $200, is an excellent, reasonably priced way to create progressive frames.

13. **Shoot at 24fps if you have the option.** Cameras that shoot true 24fps usually have their shutter open 20% longer per frame, which means that more light data is being recorded. As many of the keyers designed for DV/HDV/HD footage combine luma and chroma data, the more data you can record on both levels, the better the key they can produce. Just keep Rule No. 11 in mind, because motion blur makes your subject difficult to key. A good compromise is shooting 24fps at 1/48 shutter speed.

14. **If you can shoot at a higher resolution than your project demands, do so.** Obviously, the greater the resolution your camera can record, the more data for the keyer to work with afterward. The huge benefit to shooting at a higher resolution than what you will output is that you can key at the higher resolution and then shrink the image to fit the output resolution. This will give you much more precision and make minor keying artifacts virtually unnoticeable. The higher resolution will also allow you to pan across a larger space in post.

15. **Don't shoot greenscreen with a 35mm adapter.** If you've read any of the articles, critiques, or reviews at *MicroFilmmaker* Magazine, you're probably aware that we love the film look a 35mm adapter can provide. However, for greenscreen work, you want your subject to have sharp, clean, in-focus edges. Once you've keyed your subject cleanly, then you can create the look of shallow depth of field in post with out-of-focus backgrounds and feathered focus edges on your subject.

16. **Whenever possible, make sure you have a laptop with some sort of video editing/previewing software on it.** Doing so will allow you to check your background pictures while you're lighting to make sure things are set up properly. Adobe's Ultra actually enables you to see exactly what the key will look like live with your background. With most editing software packages, you can record a few seconds of footage, composite it in your favorite keyer, and thereby make sure your lighting will blend with the background. If you have Adobe OnLocation on your laptop, you can use the light meter software that's part of it to check all your lighting levels and label your clips on the fly; and it can also record true 24fps progressive with the DVX100, HVX200A, and certain other 24p cameras. ScopeBox allows you to do the same things on a Mac laptop.

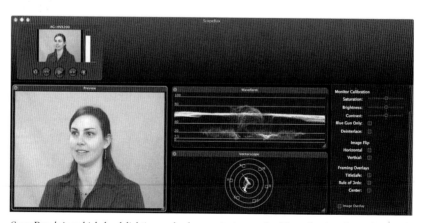

ScopeBox brings high-level lighting and color monitoring to the Mac, allowing cleaner keys to be obtained in production. Printed with permission of ScopeBox.

5 things to prep your talent with for optimal shoots

Beyond these main rules to shoot by, I would be remiss if I didn't also leave you with some information about working with your talent. Even if you follow all 16 of the main rules perfectly, you can run into problems if you don't take the following steps with your talent.

1. **Don't have your talent show up until you have most of the greenscreen set up.** Unless you have a permanent greenscreen studio, you should plan on at least two to four hours to set up a greenscreen and light it properly for the first time. You don't want your talent hanging around getting bored, tired, and cranky. And you don't want them to get hot and sweaty, as we cover in No. 4.

2. **Make sure your talent wears nothing that is green or is largely a green derivative.** Several colors, like teal and aqua, are blends of blue and green and are thus bad choices for your talent to wear. Beware of getting tunnel vision about avoiding just green. Additionally, some colors tend to reflect or pick up green unduly; for some reason, khakis and browns can attract a green coloration. If you're using a bluescreen, obviously you should make sure that your actors avoid blue/green clothes and traditional blue clothes like jeans.

3. **Make sure your actors aren't wearing anything shiny and that there's nothing shiny in the physical set.** Shiny things reflect green and will thus become transparent. Matte clothes are best for actors, and matte finishes for any pieces of furniture. Even glossy wood furniture can reflect green, so you can imagine what happens with stainless steel furniture and glass tabletops. Watch out also for props like water bottles, crystal balls, and reading glasses.

4. **Make sure you have fresh makeup on your actors at all times.** While makeup is necessary for any film endeavor to get the look you want, it's extremely important for greenscreen as it prevents your actors from becoming shiny and reflecting greenscreen light. The intensity of the lighting for greenscreen can cause makeup to melt off at a faster rate than in other types of shoots. Plan on having the makeup refreshed regularly.

5. **Try to have your actors' hair as styled as possible.** One of the most difficult things about greenscreen is keying feathery hair,

which tends to occur when hair is messed up or hanging naturally. Remember that we're trying to get clean edges, so style your actors' hair as tight as possible. If it's appropriate to the character, use gel for a slicked-down look, or a tight braid — or even a shaved head. Everyone's needs are different in filmmaking, but a convenient hairstyle is easy enough to plan ahead for.

CHAPTER 11: KEYING ESSENTIALS

Go from a greenscreen shot to a beautiful moody composite. Greenscreen footage courtesy of Angie Mistretta. 3D background courtesy of Paul Wood.

There are many truths about keying. Keying is a science and an art. Keying is trial and error. You will never get a perfect key in a single pass. There is no such thing as a perfect key.

Think of this half of the book as Keying 101. There are other books on compositing that go extremely deeply into the science behind pulling a good key, measuring exact colors and throwing algebraic equations at you. I promise not to go too geeky on you. The goal of this text is to allow you to absorb as much information as you can in the shortest amount of time. You will learn to key properly using nonlinear editors (NLEs) and compositing tools with which you already have familiarity. Why waste your time with algebra?

In this part of the book, you will learn some of the terminology and basic workflow of keying, including how to prepare your footage and work with multiple masks. We will cover keyers for Adobe After Effects and Apple Final Cut Studio, as well as terrific third-party plug-ins to help you get the job done better and faster.

Great keying technique vs. good storytelling

Our focus, of course, is to explain keying technique and many of the ways that you can achieve realistic results in your composite. It is very important to remember, though, that a great key cannot replace good storytelling. If your story isn't compelling, no amount of CGI and effects will fix it. Every summer a boatload of films that are basically effects extravaganzas come out and many have incredibly well-done effects, but the stories lack focus, heart, good dialogue, and so on. Don't be that person who makes the next *Alien vs. Predator* or *Leonard Part 6* — please!

CHAPTER 12: PREPARE YOUR FOOTAGE

Bryan Kezer, who hosted a now-defunct community Web site that focused on creating and delivering tutorials for Pinnacle Impression DVD software, has some rules about working with greenscreen and production in general:

Rule No. 1: Garbage in, garbage out.

Rule No. 2: Measure twice, cut once.

Rule No. 3: People who say "Fix it in post" are probably terrorists and shouldn't be trusted, because ...

Rule No.4: We can't fix everything in post.

Rule No. 1 translates to: "If your footage looks crappy, it will be tough to key." Rule No. 2 is not so much of an issue with NLEs. Rule No. 4, however, is the rule that most of us do not want to face. Even if you've followed every rule about shooting greenscreen, you will still inevitably end up with something that needs to be fixed, whether it be green spill created by the camera or compression issues from DV. Correcting the footage before the key will save you a lot of time and frustration. Here's a quick to-do list that you should go over with each greenscreen shot.

1. Check pixel aspect ratio
2. Deinterlace footage
3. Denoise and deartifact footage
4. Check your edges
5. Even out your greenscreen
6. Create garbage (junk) mattes

Check pixel aspect ratio/frame aspect ratio

Pixel aspect ratio (PAR) is one of those confusing technical things that can cause big problems if you are not careful. You just have to know how to work with it, not the entire science behind it.

Most computer screens have a frame aspect ratio of 4:3 and use square pixels with a 1:1 pixel aspect ratio — the pixels are as tall as they are wide. NTSC DV and D1 video also have a frame aspect ratio of 4:3, but they use non-square pixels. Non-square video pixels are stretched tall. When viewed on a computer screen they look fat. When they're output to video, though, they once again appear correct.

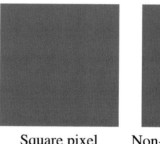

Non-square pixels look skinnier than square pixels.

**Square pixel
1.0 PAR**

**Non-Square pixel
0.9 PAR**

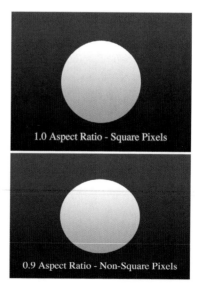

1.0 Aspect Ratio - Square Pixels

0.9 Aspect Ratio - Non-Square Pixels

This is how non-square pixels will appear on your computer.

To adjust the pixel aspect ratio in Adobe After Effects, go to File > Interpret Footage Main, and change the settings in the pull-down menu.

Each footage item has its PAR, which can be modified in the Interpret Footage dialog box in After Effects. After Effects will set your footage up correctly so long as your video is tagged properly and no one has messed with the settings. If this is set up incorrectly, your video will look stretched and your actors will look fat. Trust me, they won't appreciate it.

After Effects will also allow you to composite with different PARs in a single composition. If you have set up a composition with square pixels and drag a DV clip into your timeline, it will automatically convert the non-square video to square pixels.

After Effects also has built-in pixel aspect ratio correction. At the bottom of your Comp window, there is a little button to Toggle Pixel Aspect Ratio Correction. After Effects will preview everything in your comp window as square pixels, so it looks correct to your eye, which really does make it much easier to work with.

Toggle Pixel Aspect Ratio Correction.

Deinterlace **your fields**

Most video has two separate fields that constitute a single interlaced frame of video. These fields are interweaved, alternating lines of image in order to smooth out motion and reduce flicker.

	Frame Rate	Field Rate
NTSC	29.97 fps	59.94 fields/sec

The standard frame rate in television is 60 interlaced fields (60i, which is technically 59.94) for NTSC and 50 interlaced fields (50i) for PAL and

SECAM. These standards have been used for decades. Old televisions couldn't keep up with footage that had a lot of action, so fields were introduced to help the flickering problem resulting from slow-drawing pictures on the TV. Interlacing does allow video to play back more smoothly, but each field has only half the resolution. We've come a long way with our big flat-screen televisions that hang on the wall, yet interlaced fields are still in use everywhere.

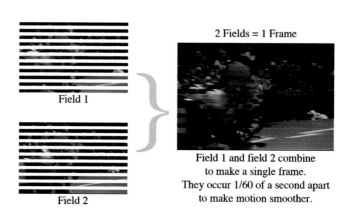

Field 1

Field 2

2 Fields = 1 Frame

Field 1 and field 2 combine to make a single frame. They occur 1/60 of a second apart to make motion smoother.

Computers have progressive displays, so fields can cause a lot of problems if you're working with video on a computer. They're most noticeable in areas of fast camera movement, motion blur, and along contrasting edges. They can make keying more difficult and if you scale your video, the problem gets even worse. If you are keying, masking, scaling, or performing any number of similar procedures, you need to deinterlace your footage before you do anything else.

The horizontal "comb-teeth" lines across the video are fields. Scaling footage that is not deinterlaced properly causes field issues to become much worse.

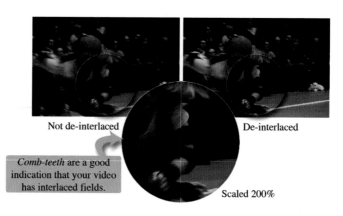

Not de-interlaced

De-interlaced

Comb-teeth are a good indication that your video has interlaced fields.

Scaled 200%

Deinterlacing is the process of removing the interlacing. If you've shot your video in progressive (i.e., no fields, only frames), you can skip this part. Lucky you.

Deinterlacing fields in After Effects. Here is the step-by-step procedure for deinterlacing in Adobe After Effects.

1. Look at your footage to determine if you have fields. You will see the "comb-teeth" lines if interlaced fields are present. Look at a minimum of five frames because the interlacing may not be obvious — your footage may not have a lot of movement or may have been transferred from film and 3:2 pull-down was used. Flash files, 3D renders, and film captures do not have fields, and deinterlacing them will only reduce resolution.

2. Determine the field order. It's critical that you use the correct field order or your fields will be reversed, resulting in a big stripy mess. After Effects will automatically detect whether your footage is lower or upper field first, but if the video isn't tagged with this information, you'll have to determine the field order and deinterlace yourself.

   After Effects uses interpretation rules to guess at field order:
   • All DV footage is lower fields first.
   • NTSC D1 footage will depend on the hardware.
   • Interlaced HD footage is lower field first.
   • PAL D1 is upper field first.

   After Effects should deinterlace only the moving areas of the video. It's not an exact science, though, and doesn't respond well to some kinds of footage.

3. Select your footage in the Project window.

4. Go to File > Interpret Footage > Main. Go to the Fields and Pull-down section. Choose Lower Field First or Upper Field First. The shortcut for the Interpret Footage Main window is Option+double click (Alt+double click).

5. View footage in the Footage window to view after deinterlacing. Double-click on the footage in your timeline and Opt/Alt+double click to open it in the Footage window. Use the Page Down key to tap through frame by frame. If the motion looks jumpy and doesn't flow smoothly in sequence, your field order is probably wrong. If it's wrong, repeat Step 4. (Note: If you double-click the footage in the Project window, it plays in the QuickTime player, before the deinterlacing.)

Once in a while you'll get footage that is screwed up — probably scaled without deinterlacing, then rendered again. You must not deinterlace footage that is mangled in this way. You can try doing nothing with the fields and hopefully no one will notice, but the best solution is to get ahold of the original footage, before it was messed up, and start over.

Third-party solutions for dealing with fields. RE:Vision Effects FieldsKit ($89.95) provides smarter deinterlacing and better workflow options for interlacing and pull-down. FieldsKit works with Adobe After

Effects, Adobe Premiere Pro, Apple Final Cut Pro, Autodesk Combustion, and other After Effects-compatible products.

Red Giant Magic Bullet Frames ($199.00) is another third-party choice. Start with ordinary interlaced video, apply Magic Bullet Frames with its sophisticated algorithms, and you'll get the smoother, professional deinterlaced look of 24p film.

You can learn more about fields and deinterlacing from Cybermotion, run by Chris and Trish Meyer. They have a great video training series about fields in After Effects that is available at *Lynda.com*.

Denoise and deartifact

You will get much cleaner keys if you first reduce artifacting, noise, and grain in your footage, and smooth your color channels. This pre-process may not be necessary if you have awesome footage, but if you're shooting DV, a quick cleanup will help your key look measurably cleaner.

Noise from poor lighting, JPEG and other compression-induced artifacting, film grain, and halftone patterns are just a few types of noise that you might want to remove. In DV footage, blue will almost always be the noisiest channel and green the cleanest channel.

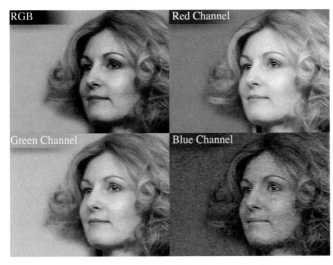

The noise in DV is very harsh in the blue channel in this example.

*Footage tip. If you can afford to upgrade to an HD camera with its higher color space and lower compression, do so. The less compression you have, the easier it is to key. With DV and HDV footage, you'll need to clean up more noise and artifacting.

Reducing noise per channel. My friend Angie Mistretta, visual effects artist and Apple Shake guru, has this advice about reducing noise that applies to pretty much any host application: "Be sure to degrain your footage via each channel." Sometimes a soft blur on the blue channel will take care of your problem, but do so very carefully. Most of the time, that won't be enough. Angie adds, "If you need to shift channels, degrain each one and then reunite the channels. Shake has a node that will allow you to tune for each individual channel." So, how do you do this with After Effects?

The Remove Grain filter in Adobe After Effects. To degrain per channel, try the Remove Grain plug-in that ships with After Effects. It can soften your footage if you adjust the settings too high, but in small doses it can do wonders.

1. Apply Effect > Noise & Grain > Remove Grain. Remove Grain does a great job of figuring out the algorithm behind the noise and removing it.

2. Remove Grain and several third-party plug-ins have a Preview Area, which is a white box that shows you a sample of the plug-in at the current settings. This helps speed up rendering and screen redraw. By clicking and dragging the center point of the preview region, you can drag it to the area that you want to use as reference.

3. Under the Noise Reduction Settings > Mode, you can specify whether you want to reduce noise in all channels (multichannel) or

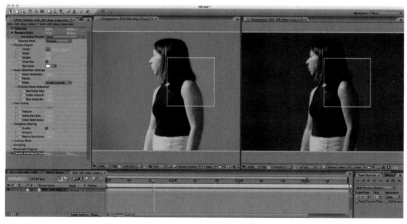

The Preview Area is the white box. It's shown with dual Composition windows with RGB (left) and the blue channel (right). Footage (here and on following pages) courtesy of Tom Stern, FILMdyne Productions, LLC

in one channel at a time (single channel). Because noise in video is mainly in the blue channel, the noise reduction for the blue channel can be set higher than the other channels.

4. When reducing noise it's helpful to see both the combined RGB and a single channel so you don't have to switch back and forth between channels. Do this by opening two Composition windows side by side, which will serve a number of other purposes too. (See the instructions for opening a second Comp window on page 72.)

5. Remove Grain doesn't work well with dirt or dust on video because it works with the full frame of video. You can adjust the sampling points under the Sampling menu. The sample points should be placed in an area of midtonal ranges with no natural texture, such as over trees, water, or a stucco wall. Remove Grain will calculate the noise based on the texture and will not help your cause. Mark Christiansen's book *Adobe After Effects CS3 Professional Studio Techniques* talks about the Remove Grain plug-in used to give an aging actress a tighter face, so occasionally using this plug-in for a digital Botox on a skin texture can be very helpful! By default, the sampling points are taken from the first frame. You can adjust and keyframe the source frame also.

The Remove Grain sampling points.

6. Adjust the Noise Reduction settings and the Fine Tuning in Remove Grain. Be careful not to be too heavy-handed with the effect because it will flatten your textures. Before rendering, switch the Viewing mode to Final Output.

For removing noise specifically for keying, many keyers have built-in noise suppression. The Foundry Keylight has Screen Pre-Blur and Screen Softness options.

Open a second Comp viewer for better monitoring. To open a second Composition viewer in After Effects, click on the title of your composition at the top of your comp viewer. A pull-down will appear. Select New Comp Viewer. Drag the new composition tab to the right side of the Comp Viewer window until it highlights purple, then let go of the mouse button. To change the channel being viewed for the New Comp Viewer, use Show Channel at the bottom of the Comp window.

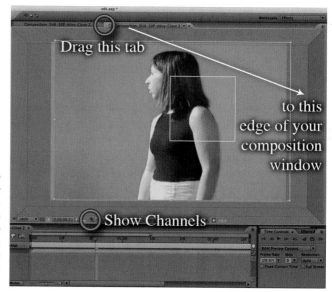

Having two Comp windows with the same composition can speed up workflow because you don't have to keep flipping back and forth between views.

Third-party solutions for reducing noise. When I talked to Peter Litwinowicz, cofounder of RE:Vision Effects, in 2008 at NAB — an enormous broadcast trade show in Las Vegas — he told me: "Noise in the greenscreen areas can hamper your ability to pull a great key. DE:Noise is a great plug-in to help pull a better key, because it helps eliminate noise while keeping sharp the details and edges of your objects of interest."

RE:Vision Effects DE:Noise ($149) works with several host applications, including Adobe After Effects, Adobe Premiere Pro, Boris Red, Autodesk Combustion, Apple Final Cut Pro, Apple Motion, and eyeon Fusion.

Digital Film Tools Composite Suite ($295) includes a plug-in called Deartifact, which is handy for cleaning up artifacts caused by DV and HD video footage. In fact, it's particularly useful for cleaning up images that have aliased or jaggy edges.

Boris FX, Inc. offers Continuum Complete ($899), which is more expensive than the other plug-ins we've mentioned but has everything, including two noise removal filters: BCC DeGrain Filter and BCC DeNoise Filter. BCC DeGrain removes grain from footage by analyzing a grain sample and removing noise of a similar frequency and amplitude. The BCC DeNoise is especially useful when restoring film, because it can correct dark areas that were created by film emulsion or video compression. BCC is available for just about every host application you might use.

Lastly, Red Giant Software Key Correct Pro ($399), which is a powerhouse for greenscreen work, is made specifically for keying and quickly cleaning up noisy footage and mattes. The Denoiser and Alpha Cleaner tools do a bang-up job of fixing noise problems in poorly lit footage.

Check your edges

Once you have either toned down or removed the grain, check the edges of your foreground subject. If they're stair-steppy, jaggy, aliased edges — and they probably are if you shot DV — your key will not look smooth. DV compressed footage, as you already know, has downsampled color channels, which means that the jaggies will be even more noticeable after you pull your key.

Smoothing edges with Channel Combiner and Channel Blur in After Effects. My good friend Angie, who helped me out tremendously on this book, taught me a great trick that she learned from her instructors. It involves shifting the color space of your video to YUV in After Effects.

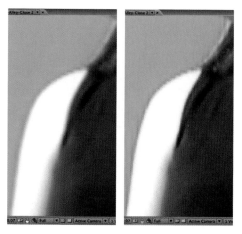

The example on the left used the Channel Combiner to convert RGB to YUV and back. The sample on the right used Channel Blur only.

1. In After Effects, shift the color space of the footage to YUV by applying the Channel Combiner effect (Effect > Channel > Channel Combiner). Use the From pull-down menu to change from RGB to YUV. Your footage will look really bizarre, but that's normal. Please note: This plug-in only supports 8bpc (bits per channel), not 16bpc. If you're working in 16bpc, you will get an error message telling you that "Using this effect in 16 bit per channel project may reduce color precision."

2. Add a slight horizontal blur on only the red and blue channels. To do this, apply Channel Blur (Effect > Blur & Sharpen > Channel Blur). Don't blur too much because you don't want your image to look soft. Be gentle! Check the Repeat Edge Pixels box and set the Blur Dimensions to Horizontal.

3. You may also need to add a slight vertical blur. If so, repeat the process above with a new instance of Channel Blur. The vertical blur will need to be much less than the horizontal blur.

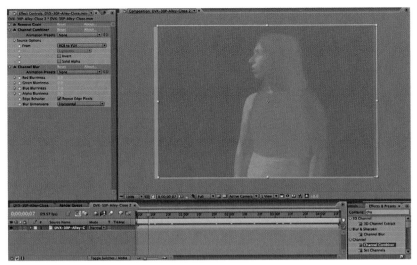

Channel Combiner was applied and the footage is converted from RGB to YUV. A slight Channel Blur on the red and blue channels has been added to soften the edges.

4. Convert back to RGB by applying the Channel Combiner again. You can just duplicate the effect in your Effect Controls window, drag it below the Channel Blur effect, and then change the From to YUV to RGB.

5. You may not notice much of a difference, but zoom in a bit and turn off both of your Channel Combiner effects. You'll see there's a huge difference.

Why do you need to convert to YUV? The YUV color model, technically YCbCr, is used in composite color video standards. The best explanation I've seen is from Wikipedia: "The use of YCbCr also allows you to perform lossy subsampling with the chroma channels (typically to 4:2:2 or 4:1:1 ratios), which aids to reduce the resultant file size."

What does that mean? Here is the YUV color space breakdown:

Y (or Luma) = 30% Red + 59% Green + 11% Blue luminance

U (or Cb)= R − Y, the red signal minus the luminance

V (or Cr) = B − Y, the blue signal minus the luminance

Notice that green is by far the largest portion of the Y channel, which explains why greenscreen works best for video.

Third-party solutions for smoothing jaggy edges. Red Giant Key Correct Pro, a plug-in for Adobe After Effects, contains a plug-in called Deartifactor, which is very easy to use. Apply Deartifactor before your keyer, since this is a pre-process filter. Set your color mode and it automatically helps with blockiness. You can specify your color mode: DV, HDCAM, or Other.

Digital Film Tools zMatte, which is covered in more detail in the third-party keyers section, includes a plug-in called Deartifact. Deartifact is great for cleaning up artifacts caused by DV and HD video footage, as well as those aliased or jaggy edges.

dvMatte Pro Studio from dvGarage ($199) does this whole edge-smoothing process automatically with its Edge Blending controls. dvMatte Pro Studio works in Apple Final Cut Pro, Final Cut Express, and Motion.

Even out your greenscreen

If your footage is somewhat dark in the edges and the greenscreen is unevenly lit, try doing a bit of pre-key color correction to smooth out your color channels. Use Hue/Saturation or Curves (both effects are under Effect > Color Correction in After Effects CS3 and above). Push the greens up just a touch. You will only want to try this if there is very little green or spill on your actor.

Picking up green in the eyes

The image on the left shows the original footage with noisy background, as well as the Effect control panel settings for Red Giant Key Correct Pro Deartifactor and Smooth Screen. The center image shows the results of Smooth Screen. Notice how the foreground image has not been affected. The image on the right shows View Strength, the area where the noise is being cleaned up. Footage courtesy of Natsuki Kato.

Third-party solutions for evening out your greenscreen

Red Giant Key Correct Pro Smooth Screen does an excellent job of removing noise and unevenness in the background color by averaging pixels. Again, apply before your keyer, as this is a pre-process filter. There are adjustment sliders for controlling the level of Screen Color, Hue Tolerance, Lightness Tolerance, and Flattening.

If you receive footage from someone else and they compressed the heck out of it, Key Correct Pro works incredibly well to get rid of the compression noise. If you view Screen Mode > View Strength, the white pixels show the area where the noise is being smoothed. This is a very nice way of actually seeing exactly where the cleaning is being done. Be careful not to be too heavy-handed with the effect because it can tint your foreground and eat away at areas with motion blur.

dvMatte Pro Studio has a feature called Screen Fix that cleans the greenscreen for you by using a clean plate. Always shoot a clean plate, or a shot of the background without the talent in it. dvMatte Pro Studio works in Apple Final Cut Pro and Motion.

Save an animation pre-set of your pre-process effects

If you're doing a lot of keying in Adobe After Effects, I recommend setting up an animation pre-set that automates the processes we've covered so far. Include a Remove Grain effect, the Convert to YUV/Blur Edges/ Convert to RGB method and a Smooth Screen effect. It's very easy to set this up, and it will speed up your work. You'll just need to tweak the effects after they are applied to suit your footage. This technique works best when applied to shots that were filmed under the same lighting and with the same camera, but they can always be tweaked.

1. In your Effect Controls window, select all of the pre-process effects that you have applied. You may want to remove any keyframes that have been set just for the purpose of saving the pre-set.

2. Go to Animation > Save Animation Pre-set. In the dialog box, name the pre-set. It will have a .ffx extension.

Saving your pre-process effects and settings as an After Effects preset will save time and work, if you have several shots that were shot with the same camera and light settings.

3. To apply your pre-set, select a new greenscreen shot. Go to Animation > Apply Animation Pre-set, and navigate to your saved pre-set. Click Open.

4. Modify the settings to suit this shot.

5. Note: If there were keyframes in your original saved pre-set, the keyframes will be applied starting at the frame where you applied the pre-set to your footage.

Garbage mattes (aka junk mattes)

Now that you have prepared your footage, there is one last task we must take care of before we start to key: garbage mattes.

Normal keying workflow involves applying a garbage matte before applying the keyer. Professionals never key without a garbage matte.

A garbage matte is a loose animated mask around your foreground footage to exclude areas of your footage you do not want to keep, like uneven greenscreen lighting, shadows, tracking dots, props, wires, and rigging.

Garbage mattes limit the amount of green that your keyer will have to process, speeding up your keying process. You'll get faster keys with fewer heavy-handed adjustments.

Don't spend too much time making a perfect garbage matte that precisely outlines the subject. You're not rotoscoping. In Chapter 15 we'll talk more about an advanced technique that involves using multiple mattes to attain better keys.

Making garbage mattes in Adobe After Effects. Follow these steps to create garbage mattes in After Effects.

1. Select the Pen tool in the toolbar.

2. Click on your selected greenscreen layer to create a point.

3. Continue clicking with the Pen tool to make a full path around your foreground object.

4. You can move the points of the mask by using the Move tool (arrow in toolbar), selecting the points, and dragging them to the desired position.

The bisection method. No matter which software you're using, the fastest way to animate your garbage matte is to use the bisection method, which enables the computer to do most of the work for you by "tweening" between keyframes. Make sure you do not cut off any parts of the foreground as the actor moves around. Make a habit of scrubbing through the timeline and double-checking your masks. Here are the step-by-step instructions for the bisection method in After Effects.

★Mask tip. Make sure you start with enough points on your mask in After Effects. It's better to have a few extra than not enough. I have not had too many problems with adding points to a mask, but deleting points can be disastrous. Whatever you do, do not delete any of your mask points as you're working! Trust me on this.

Example of a garbage matte in Adobe After Effects. Footage courtesy of Natsuki Kato from the film short Thumbelina.

1. Start at the most complex frame and add your mask with the Pen tool. Clicking on the first point again will close your mask.
2. Set a keyframe for your mask. The M key brings up the mask parameters in your timeline.
3. Jump ahead one second in your timeline and adjust your mask to fit the movement in your footage. A keyframe will automatically be generated since you keyframed your first frame.
4. Jump back (bisect) to the midway point between the two keyframes (15 frames back) and adjust the mask again.
5. Check the points in between and make adjustments to the matte where necessary. If the mask is cutting off something important, simply drag it to the right place.

★Mask tip: Always feather your masks! You do not want to have any hard edges that might show in your composite. To feather in After Effects, select the layer with your mask and press the F key. This brings up the Feather option, which allows you to make your edges nice and soft.

Making garbage mattes in Apple Final Cut Pro. I've found that the mask tool in Apple Final Cut Pro is poorly implemented: You're stuck with the Four- or Eight-Point Garbage Matte, unless you use a third-party plug-in. To be blunt, I don't like using Final Cut Pro for keying specifically because the masking tools are very limited, not user-friendly, and tedious if you need to keyframe or need more points. Final Cut Pro is also inconsistent in its use of pre-multiplied alpha channels, but that's another conversation. (The limits of the masking are not unique to Final Cut Pro. Adobe Premiere Pro has the same issues, which is why many people prefer to garbage-matte and key in After Effects or Motion, both of which have better masking tools.)

Here's the basic technique for creating garbage mattes in Apple Final Cut Pro.

1. Both the Four- and Eight-Point Garbage Mattes are under Effects > Video Filters > Matte > Four- or Eight-Point Garbage Matte.
2. In the Effects window, click on the point controls and drag the crosshairs in the Canvas to where you need them.
3. Image and Overlay need to be turned on in the Canvas window to be seen.

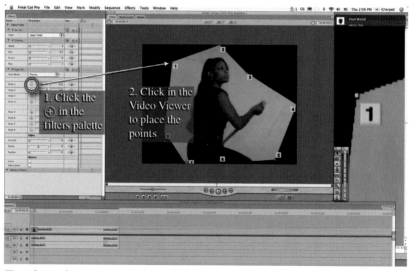

To apply a garbage matte in Apple Final Cut Pro, you need to have the Filters window open so that you can click on the crosshair, and the Viewer window open to place the points. Footage courtesy of Douglas Toltzman, Oak Street Software.

4. It helps to have your window open nice and wide so that you can see all of the points clearly. It also helps to zoom in to get into those tight spaces.

5. Keyframe if needed.

6. Set the View mode to Final when you're finished.

Third-party options for garbage matte creation in Apple Final Cut Pro. You do have a couple of options if you need more points on your mask in Final Cut Pro. You can overlap mattes, but that can be a painful process, especially if you are keyframing them. Third-party filters once again come to the rescue. If you have to use Final Cut Pro for keying, you can generate a garbage matte with 2 to 40 points that have bezier handles with CHV Bezier Garbage Matte Pro ($49). This tool is more of a path tool for Final Cut Pro and also lets you stroke the path, blur the matte, rotate, scale, and perform other transformations, so it's not just a one-trick pony. CHV Bezier Garbage Matte Pro is FxScript and also works in Final Cut Express. Another option is Paul Crisp FCP Garbage Mattes, a free garbage matte tool for Final Cut Pro, which is available at *kenstone3.net/ fcp_homepage/paul_crisp_garbage_mattes.sit.*

If you really want to key in Final Cut Pro, a good option is to draw your garbage masks in Apple Motion, save your Motion project, and then open it in Final Cut Pro. All of your masks will remain intact.

Making garbage mattes in Apple Motion. I may be down on Final Cut Pro's masks, but Apple Motion is a terrific program for working with greenscreen footage. Motion handles masks much better than Final Cut Pro, and you can use FxPlug keyers and go back and forth between Motion and Final Cut Pro without rendering. Motion also has real-time previews and in my opinion is just much more user-friendly overall.

1. Bring your greenscreen footage onto your canvas.

2. Make sure your greenscreen layer is selected.

3. Motion gives you several mask tools, which are stored under two mask icons with pull-down menus at the top of the toolbar. The one on the left contains a rectangle, an oval, and a very cool Freeform vector mask-drawing tool. The Freeform tool allows you to create articulated (hand-drawn) masks easily and works even better with a Wacom tablet. The second icon contains bezier pen tools.

4. Click on the canvas with your pen to make your garbage matte. Make sure you close your path and feather your mask by clicking on the Mask tab under the Inspector and dragging the Feather slider.

The Freeform Mask Tool in Motion allows for very fast articulated mattes. Footage courtesy of Douglas Toltzman, Oak Street Software.

CHAPTER 13: GETTING TO KNOW THE KEYERS

Remember, you will not be able to get a perfect key in a single pull, no matter how advanced a keyer you use. You must help the keyer with procedural mattes and core mattes and a few passes of the keyer with separate areas masked off. But before we get into those complex techniques, let's finish going over keyers.

★Keying tip. Daniel Land of Unit Circle Films has a great tip for any keying job: "A lot of times it helps to start on the most difficult frame in the shot, one that has the worst shadows or holes, then work outward from there. Tackle the toughest part first and then it's all downhill."

An overview of some keying plug-ins in Adobe After Effects

After Effects ships with several built-in keyers. I'll go over a few of them.

Your basic Color Key. Several NLEs and compositing programs have built-in chromakeying tools; the most basic is the Color Key. Most NLEs have a similar Color Key that works in the same general way. The After Effects Color Key has the following parameters that you can adjust:

- Key Color: Choose the color you want to remove and the Color Key removes that color.
- Color Tolerance: Add or remove varying shades of your key color.
- Edge Thin: Contract or expand your mask one pixel at a time.
- Edge Feather: Soften the matte.

After Effects Color Key doesn't have many bells and whistles and doesn't work very well with hair or anything fuzzy.

After Effects Color Key applied with a garbage matte. Footage courtesy of Unit Circle Productions from the film Dirty Trousers.

*Keying tip. Change the background color of your composition to a contrasting color so that you can see the edges and transparency in your key. Alternately, place a full-frame contrasting-color solid behind your keyed layer and on top of your background plate, and toggle it on and off as needed. You'll be able to see your key as you work.

Color Difference Keyer. After Effects has a more powerful, but somewhat confusing, keyer called the Color Difference Keyer (CDK). It was the best keyer in After Effects before The Foundry's Keylight was included. It works fairly well on hair and there is an option to feather edges of the matte.

1. Apply the Color Difference Keyer: Effects > Keying > Color Difference Keyer.

2. I find it's easiest to work with this plug-in if I set the view to Matte Corrected (the alpha matte). This will give you the black-and-white alpha channel in your Composition window. You can also see it in the preview in the Effect Controls window.

3. Use the top eyedropper between the thumbnails, or the dropper called Color Key, and choose a shade of green very close to your actor.

4. Below the preview you'll notice the letters A, B, and a character that looks like a cursive "a" and stands for alpha matte. To break this down, the A + B are two different mattes, a primary and secondary matte, that are blended together to give you an alpha matte. Partial A is based on your foreground. Partial B is based on the background or your greenscreen.

5. Select Partial A by clicking on the A square below the thumbnail. Use the black eyedropper (center eyedropper) to select the lightest shade of black in the thumbnail.

6. Select Partial B by clicking on the B square. Use the black eyedropper again, and sample an area of the greenscreen. Most of the background will hopefully be gone by this point.

7. Adjust the Partial A and B levels by first adjusting the values for In Black and In White. These work a lot like the Levels effect. By increasing the black values for In Black, you darken your blacks, adding more transparency. White is exactly the opposite. When you decrease white values for In White, you brighten your whites and add opaqueness.

8. Reduce the contrast by increasing the Out Black and Out White.

9. Set the view to Final Output and then adjust the Matte Gamma as needed. Matte Gamma adjusts midtones only.

The Color Difference Keyer is not very intuitive but works well on hair and other nonsmooth-edged objects.

10. You'll most likely have a green halo around the edges. Applying a Spill Suppressor will take care of some of the spillage (Effect > Keying > Spill Suppressor) by tinting the green edges. Despill is discussed at greater length on page 115. A matte choker will also help.

Luma Key. Luma keys work best for objects shot over white with very little white in the foreground image. Sometimes a luma key works well for removing a white sky so that you can replace it with something prettier. After Effects Luma Key has the following options:

Luma Key leaves a thin white edge around the subject, which was shot over white. A matte choker would help with the edge. Image courtesy of iStockPhoto.com.

- Key Type: Key Out Brighter, Key Out Darker, Key Out Similar, Key Out Dissimilar
- Threshold
- Tolerance
- Edge Thin
- Edge Feather

In my experience, Luma Key hasn't been all that flexible and I rarely use it. It's difficult to get a clean edge without eating into your foreground. I wanted to bring it up because it's very tempting to want to key fire or an explosion that is shot over black, but there is a better way.

If you have something like smoke or fire shot over black-and-white, check out Chapter 18 under "Key smoke and fire? Not!"

Inner/Outer Keys. The Inner/Outer Key is more work than most of the other keyers because it uses masks, but the results are stellar. This keyer works great on hair and anything fuzzy. I've had very good luck even with a non-greenscreen and non-contrasty background. This is easiest with footage that doesn't move much, like a talking head or a tree sloth.

There are a couple of tricks to using the Inner/Outer Keyer. Here are the basics, along with the tricks

1. Bring your footage into After Effects and draw an Outer mask outside the edge of your foreground object. Make sure it's fairly tight but not right at the edges. (Remember, this is not a rotoscope.) Be sure to close your mask. Also, set your Mask mode to None, so that you can see what you are doing.

2. Rename your Outer mask by selecting your layer and tapping the M key to bring up the Mask parameter in your timeline. Select the mask and click the Return/Enter key, which will make the mask name editable. Type the name "Outer" and press return. It's important that you name it Outer because the Inner/Outer Key is looking for that name and will automatically assign the mask to the right area of the plug-in.

3. Create an Inner mask, this time drawing just inside the edges of your foreground object. Rename it Inner.

4. A quick way to make your Inner mask is to duplicate your Outer mask, then grab the points and scale it in. You'll save about 75% of the time doing it this way. Of course, if your clip is long and you're setting a lot of keyframes because of a lot of movement, this could get messy.

5. It's helpful to change the color of your mask, especially if you need to create several masks (see Chapter 15, "Automatically cycle mask colors in After Effects"). You may need more than inner and outer masks if you have areas that need to be cut out of your object, such as the area around a bent elbow.

The Inner/Outer Key works great with fur and hair. Image courtesy of iStockPhoto.com.

6. Apply the Inner/Outer Key (Effects > Keying > Inner/Outer Key). Since you named your masks Inner and Outer, the correct masks should be automatically applied in the effect. If nothing happens when you apply the effect, switch the Inner and Outer pull-downs to the opposite settings. You should immediately see the background go away.

7. Draw in Additional Foreground and Additional Background masks if needed. In the sample, this is the hole between the arm and the body. Select the Additional Background and Additional Foreground masks in the pull-down menu in the Effect Controls window.

8. Set up Clean Up Foreground and Background masks if needed. They work in the same general way. Adjust the Edge Thin, Feather, and Threshold as needed.

CHAPTER 14: AN OVERVIEW OF SOME THIRD-PARTY PLUG-INS

Some low-budget filmmakers and hobbyists I've talked to refuse to buy plug-ins. They claim that they shouldn't have to spend money on something that comes "out of the box" with Adobe After Effects. Sorry, I don't agree with that logic at all. Not every tool in After Effects can handle the job. Some lack the power or the flexibility that third-party plug-ins can bring to the task. Time is money, and spending extra on a plug-in makes a lot of sense if it will be much easier, give you a better result, speed up your workflow drastically — and most important, keep you from ripping out your hair. Life is short, after all.

For a long time, plug-ins worked only in a single host application — two if you were lucky. If the plug-in was available on multiple hosts, you had to buy multiple licenses. Many plug-ins have evolved to work with many different hosts, especially now that Apple has migrated to Intel processors and FxPlug. FxPlug is a technology developed by Apple that allows plug-ins to be shared between Final Cut Pro and Motion, and they are also GPU accelerated. Several plug-ins that were once available for only After Effects now work in Premiere Pro, Final Cut Pro, Motion, and even Avid.

I won't demonstrate how to use the plug-ins in each host, but I'll give an overview of each of the plug-ins and how it works. They work much the same way in each host, so it shouldn't be a problem if I'm demonstrating in Apple Final Cut Pro or Motion and you're using Adobe After Effects.

Here is a list of the plug-ins that I'll cover, several of which work in multiple host applications:

- The Foundry Keylight
- Red Giant Primatte Keyer Pro
- Oak Street Software VKey2
- Digital Film Tools zMatte

The Foundry Keylight

Keylight from The Foundry is a favorite among visual effects artists, because it is easy to use and is a high-end, powerful keying tool. Keylight has shipped with the last few versions of After Effects, but it is also available for Apple Final Cut Pro, Apple Shake, Avid, Autodesk Combustion, and other Autodesk systems. It retails for $420 for a node-locked license or $630 for a floating license.

Keylight has many great features that the out-of-the-box keyers don't have, such as automatically handling spill suppression. Below is the basic setup.

1. Apply Keylight to you footage. Effects > Keying > Keylight, or drag Keylight from the Effects & Pre-sets palette onto your footage.

2. Use the eyedropper tool to grab your Screen Colour (British spelling: The Foundry is UK-based). Screen Colour is the color of your greenscreen or bluescreen. Pick the average color of your screen. Voila! It's already working.

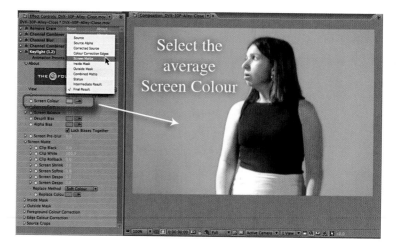

3. Change the view to Status and you'll be able to see what is being keyed out and what is being left in your foreground. Status exaggerates the alpha matte to help you locate problem areas and is not

your final alpha channel. The white area of the matte is opaque and the black area is fully transparent. The gray area is what you need to clean up.

4. Twirl down Screen Matte in your Effect Controls window and adjust the black and white clip levels, to get rid of most of the gray area. Some gray around the edges will be fine. Use this as you would the Levels control. Bringing the blacks up will make your matte more transparent and bringing the white level down will make it more opaque.

Keylight's Status shows the areas of the matte that need to be cleaned up. The image on the left was the original; the image on the right is after modification.

5. Set the view to Screen Matte, your actual alpha matte. Adjust the Screen Pre-blur, which blurs the matte before it pulls the key, making for a smoother edge. This will help improve the edges on DV footage drastically.

6. Set the view back to Final Result. Preview it and then adjust the Matte Shrink if you have some haloing around the edges of your footage. You can use negative numbers to grow your matte.

7. Bring in your background plate and position everything where you want it.

8. One great feature of Keylight is the ability to colorize your edges using Replace Colour. I've had very good results setting the Replace method to Hard Colour and using a color that blends into the background. Experiment with the settings to see what is best for your footage.

Keylight keyed footage over a 3D background. 3D footage courtesy of Paul Wood.

9.   There are also Foreground Colour Correction and Edge Colour Correction tools. Try them out. I prefer to use something more robust and specifically made for color correction. We'll talk about that later in Chapter 15 under "Color correction."

Red Giant Software Primatte Keyer Pro

Red Giant Software Primatte Keyer ($499, After Effects, Final Cut Pro, Motion, Avid Xpress Pro) has been around a very long time and is one of the pros' favorite tools. It's fast, and once you know how it works, it's very easy. It also has some nice compositing controls like Light Wrap and Color Match that really help blend your footage into the background. I will admit that it's not the most intuitive keyer on the market, but that's why I'm going to give you this overview on how to use it.

I'm going to walk you through using Primatte Keyer Pro in Adobe After Effects, but it's pretty similar in the other host applications. There is a free demo available at *Toolfarm.com* if you want to take Primatte Keyer Pro for a spin.

I should also mention that one of the cool things about plug-ins from Red Giant is that you buy one license and you can use it in any host application it supports on a single computer. In other words, if you have Adobe

After Effects and Apple Final Cut Pro, one license will work in both. Gotta love that!

1. Apply Primatte Keyer Pro to your footage. Effects > Primatte > Primatte Keyer Pro.

2. In the Effect Controls palette, under Deartifacting, choose your mode. The choices are DV/HDV, HDCAM, and Other. Adjust the strength slider to the best look.

3. Jump down to Selection > Select. Make sure Select BG is outlined in red to indicate that it's selected. In the Composition window, drag your mouse around on your greenscreen area to select a sample of the background. (This is the part that I didn't "get" at first.) In Apple Final Cut Pro, you sample in the Filter Controls window. Do not include any parts of your foreground object such as wispy hair. At this point, your background should be gone and you should have a rough key.

Selecting the greenscreen in Red Giant Primatte Keyer Pro. Take a sample of the background color. I didn't apply a garbage matte to the footage, but normally I would recommend it.

4. Under Keying > View, set View to Matte to see your black-and-white matte.

5. With the Sampling style set to Point, choose Clean BG. Drag your mouse arrow around any areas of the background that are not completely black. This is the area that you want to be transparent.

Take small samples. It will take a few samples to get it cleaned up properly.

6. Select Clean FG and drag your mouse arrow around the inside of your matte to sample areas that are not completely white. This is the area that you want to be opaque. Be very careful not to cross over into the transparent area. Keep sampling until it's cleaned up. Do not worry so much about the edges here. We'll take care of that shortly. It also helps to zoom in to get into tight areas.

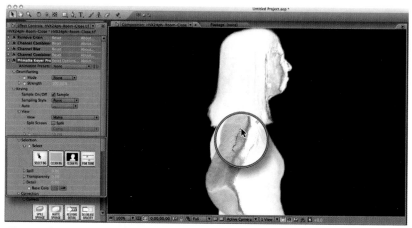

Cleaning the matte in Primatte Keyer Pro.

7. If your matte is still not tight enough, try adjusting the histogram under Alpha Controls > Gamma. It works like Levels. Drag the black arrow and your blacks are crushed. Drag the white arrow to the left and your highlights are lifted.

8. If there are holes and specks that you need to take care of in your alpha channel, twirl down Alpha Cleaner and adjust settings.

9. Switch View back to the Comp.

10. At this point you'll probably need to clean up some spill. In the Effect Controls window, click on the Spill Sponge icon. With your cursor arrow, drag your mouse around any areas that have a lot of green spill. Again, you'll want to do this in a couple of tries, not in one shot. If you have removed too much spill, undo your spill operation and sample a smaller area.

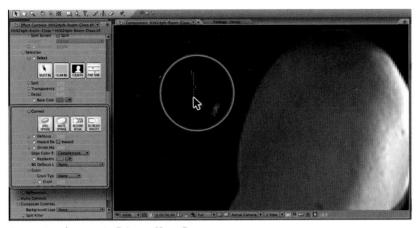

Fine-tuning the matte in Primatte Keyer Pro.

11. Time to fine-tune. If you need to dial back the spill suppression or adjust the tint, click on the Fine Tune tool under Select. Drag the slider to adjust the Spill, Transparency, and Detail.

12. To get the rest of the spill, we'll use Spill Killer under Composite Controls. First, under Composite Controls, choose your Background Layer. Then check the box next to Enable Skill Killer. Choose the Color mode, in my case, Green. Adjust the Range, Tolerance, and Strength until your green spill is gone.

13. If your edges are sharp and jaggy, you can soften your matte by adjusting Defocus Matte under Correction > Correct > Defocus Matte.

14. Primatte Keyer Pro has a great feature that allows you to tint the edges of your footage to mimic the colors of your background layer. Primatte samples the tonal range of the background layer and adjusts the foreground plate as needed. This can be fairly dramatic and gives a nice convincing composite. Scroll down to the bottom of the Primatte Keyer interface and twirl down Composite Controls > Color Matcher. Click the checkbox to Enable Color Matcher and adjust the Strength.

15. There are also settings for the Highlights, Midtones, and Shadows, which you can adjust individually to get a perfect match. All of these settings are keyframable if something changes in your shot over time. It helps to zoom in as you adjust, so that you can focus on the edges.

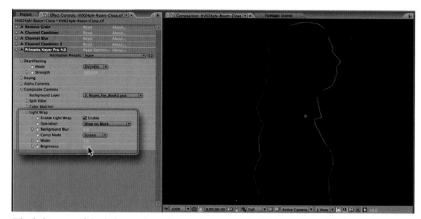

The light areas of the light wrap are shown when using the Light Wrap on Black setting.

16. The final step is to add a light wrap. A light wrap brings some of the backlighting back to the edges, to give your composite a more natural look. Twirl down the Light Wrap section of Primatte Keyer and click the checkbox to enable it.

With the examples in the Primatte Keyer Pro screen shots, a single pass of the keyer was used. As with any keyer, you will probably need to isolate and key areas with different textures individually. This technique is explained in detail in Chapter 15.

Oak Street Software VKey2

VKey2, an FxPlug vector keyer, is a new kid on the block. It is a QuickTime component that can be used in QuickTime player, Apple Final Cut Pro, Final Cut Express, Adobe Premiere, and other tools that support QuickTime effects. At the time of this writing, it has just been released as FxPlug, so it is GPU accelerated for Apple Final Cut Studio and Motion. It is specially suited to keying 4:1:1 video formats.

VKey2 is a vector keyer and works on color angles, different from a legacy chromakeyer in that it is not affected by shadows and variations in lighting. It generates a graduated key that preserves fine detail that would be lost with a traditional keyer. At $59.99, it's a steal.

I'll walk you through how to use the plug-in in Motion, because, as I mentioned earlier, the masking tools are superior to those in Final Cut Pro. But VKey2 works the same way in Final Cut Pro if that is the NLE you choose to use.

1. Bring your greenscreen footage into your NLE.

2. Create your garbage matte and do any other plate preparations that are necessary.

3. Apply VKey2 to your footage.

4. Make sure the ApplyKey box is checked.

5. Set ChromaStructure to match your source footage. For example, if you are shooting with a mini-DV, your chroma structure will be 4:1:1 for NTSC and 4:2:0 for PAL.

6. The AutoAngle checkbox is a little confusing because it's not really a switch, but more of a push-button. When activated, VKey2 samples a video frame and creates a histogram of its color values, automatically choosing the best color angle and the maximum luminance. To use AutoAngle, go to a frame in your timeline with as much of the background showing as possible, ideally on a shot of the empty screen if you shot a clean plate. Click the AutoAngle button to get the analysis started. With Motion you may have to force it to begin by moving the play head. The settings will update the respective controls automatically and the AutoAngle button will uncheck itself once the angle has been computed. The key color should be set correctly, but if it picks the wrong key color, pick a different frame with more background and repeat the process.

7. If you used AutoAngle and it worked for you, skip to step 13. If not, you must first adjust the color angle by setting the KeyRange to a low value (1 to 5 range). This will be adjusted more later.

8. Set KeyMinLumin to a very low value and the KeyMaxLumin to a very high value, so that they don't interfere with your key. These will also be tweaked later.

9. If you are not using a greenscreen, set GreenSuppress to -25, its lowest value.

10. Select Alpha > Grayscale in the Output Opts pull-down list so that you can see the black-and-white matte.

11. Select Red, Green, or Blue from the background color selector, determined by the color of your background.

12. Adjust the ColorTuning and KeyRange sliders until your matte is cleanly outlining your subject. Just as in other keying plug-ins, black equals transparency and white equals opaqueness. Leave a little bit of gray in your matte so that subtle details are not lost.

13. Adjust the feather of your edges by adjusting with the KeyFeathering slider. Low values will give you a sharper edge.

14. If you have some holes in your matte, you can use the KeyMinLumin and KeyMaxLumin sliders to define the luminance range of the background. Douglas Toltzman, owner of Oak Street Software, offers this tip: "Pixels that fall below the KeyMinLumin or exceed the KeyMaxLumin will not be keyed. By choking the luminance range of the keyer, you can save dark areas, or specular highlights in glass, for instance."

VKey2 is a vector keyer that is FxPlug, so it works in both Apple Final Cut Pro and Apple Motion, and is also a QuickTime component and works in several other host applications. Footage courtesy of Douglas Toltzman, Oak Street Software.

Useful shortcuts for working with channels in Apple Motion

- Shift + A: Show alpha channel.
- Shift + R: Show red channel.
- Shift + G: Show green channel.
- Shift + B: Show blue channel.
- Shift + C: Reset to RGB.

Digital **Film Tools zMatte**

Last but certainly not least, Digital Film Tools zMatte ($395) is a favorite of professionals everywhere. It is smart enough to zap most of the green as soon as it is applied. There's a version for Adobe After Effects and compatible programs, Apple Final Cut Pro, Avid Editing Systems, Autodesk Combustion, eyeon Digital Fusion, Autodesk Flint, Flame, Inferno, Smoke, and Fire. Now a version for Adobe Photoshop and Apple Shake is available. Okay, I think that covers pretty much everybody. A demo is available at *Toolfarm.com*.

Marco Paolini of Digital Film Tools worked in postproduction and couldn't find a keyer that fulfilled his needs, so he built one. In his own words, "Over the years of doing motion picture visual effects, the process of keying always seemed a mysterious, magical art. Our postproduction facility had every keyer available and they all seemed to work well when the green/bluescreen footage was shot properly. Unfortunately, there are only a handful of directors of photography who consistently deliver proper blue/greenscreens. The problems always arose when we received flawed footage — which was a lot of the time. All of the keyers that we used quickly failed and more often than not, we had to resort to rotoscoping. Thus, zMatte was born. We wanted a keyer that worked not only when the footage was shot well, but for those nasty blue/greenscreens as well. So we made the zMatte keyer to fit our needs. We added the features we needed to manipulate the matte, color-correct the footage, suppress spill, and make seamless composites — most of which were missing in the keyers that we were using at the time. We figured that other artists were in the same boat as us, so we decided to sell it and make it available for everyone."

zMatte is not just a keyer but has compositing tools such as Light Wrap and Color Suppress built in. Here are the basics of using zMatte in Apple Final Cut Pro.

1. Bring your greenscreen footage into Final Cut Pro. Apply zMatte Keyer. (Effects > Video Filters > DFT zMatte > zMatte Keyer).

2. Check the De-Artifact Enable (On) box. Adjust the Horizontal and Vertical Blur just below that. Gang refers to linking the horizontal and vertical together.

3. Use the Extract On pull-down menu and choose Green Screen, or something else if it's more suitable. You may already have a pretty

decent key at this point. zMatte is intelligent enough to really give you a good key without much effort.

4. Switch View from Output to Primary Matte.

5. Adjust the Background/Position until most of your background area with the greenscreen is black. Set it as high as possible so that you don't lose detail, but you want your background to be solid black.

6. Adjust the Foreground/Range to achieve a solid white foreground. Again, be gentle with the controls so you don't lose the detail.

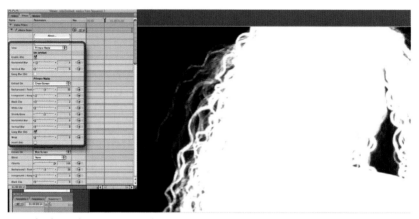

Digital Film Tools zMatte's controls in Apple Final Cut Pro, shown with the Primary Matte.

7. Adjust the Black Clip and White Clip to get rid of the gray areas of your matte.

8. Shrink/Grow, Horizontal Blur, and Vertical Blur work just as you would expect.

zMatte has an option to use a Secondary Matte, which can really help with defining edges. The instructions are in the zMatte manual. zMatte also has tools for Light Wrap, Edge, Matte Repair, and pretty much anything you need for finishing your composite.

Keyed footage in zMatte. Footage courtesy of Angie Mistretta. Background from iStockPhoto. com.

CHAPTER 15: MASTERING THE ART OF KEYING

The professionals have a toolbox of great techniques for keying that go far beyond what most beginners could imagine, and now that you know the basics of keying, I'm going to go deeper into the advanced techniques.

Aharon Rabinowitz's Super Tight Junk Mattes

Aharon has a well-known Adobe After Effects podcast and has a terrific technique called Super Tight Junk Mattes for After Effects. Because the outer areas of the greenscreen often have less-even lighting, isolating the small area around your foreground object allows you to limit the pixels that you need to remove, giving you a more precise key without compromising the edges. And it requires practically no work!

1. Apply your keyer to your greenscreen footage. It doesn't have to be that good — even the defaults will work. Just choose a color of green close to your foreground object.
2. Apply Autotrace (Layer > Autotrace).
3. In the Autotrace dialog box, check Preview so you can see the effect. Set the Time Span to Work Area. Set the Channel to Alpha. Set the threshold. If you set it at 30%, anything that is 30% opaque will be considered for the trace and anything less than 30% will be considered transparent. You want to get rid of the outer edges but keep your actor traced. Tolerance: Keep it low. I'm keeping mine at 1. Minimum Area: If I set it to 10, anything smaller than 5 x 5 pixels will be ignored. Corner Roundness: The default 50 may be okay so that it stays nice and precise around your foreground object. Check

the Apply to New Layer box so that it will create the trace on a new layer. Click OK. Tracing may take a bit of time, but trust me, doing it by hand will take much longer. Open the Info palette and it will tell you which frame is currently being traced.

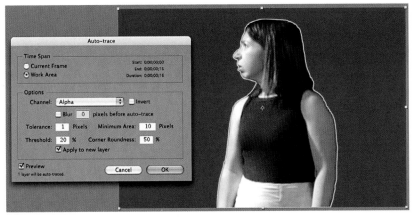

Autotrace Dialog.

4. Scrub through your footage. If it doesn't completely cover your footage, you need to expand your matte. Even just a tiny spill needs to be covered. Apply the Simple Choker to expand your matte, using negative values (Effect > Matte > Simple Choker).

5. Set the footage layer's Track Matte to Alpha so that the footage shows through the traced layer (the video layer must be just below the traced layer).

The Autotraced footage.

6. Turn off the keyer on your footage layer. Notice how you now have a thin edge of green around your footage. That is all that you will need to key out. Turn your keyer back on and adjust as necessary.

7. If there is still some stuff you're having problems getting rid of, try expanding the choke a bit more and adding a slight blur on the trace layer. It may help your footage blend into the background.

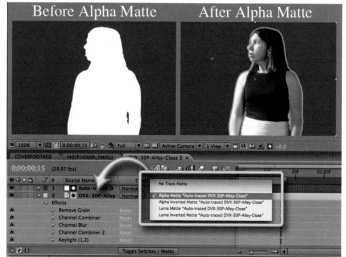

Set the Track Matte of your layer to Alpha. Track Matte is under the Modes section of your timeline.

Aharon's terrific After Effects podcasts are available at *creativecow.net/aepodcast*.

Multiple edge masks

My friend Angie Mistretta did a major keying and compositing project for her master's project at Academy of Art. She walked me through this technique that she was taught by her instructors, many of whom have worked on major motion pictures like *Star Wars*. It involves creating multiple masks to isolate certain areas of your footage to be keyed separately. You may have several keys because you have distinct types of edges. For example, hair will have one type of key while the clothing may have another. Skin tones may have different keys as well.

The other reason to use separate masks is that you will probably have to use different spill suppression settings for these dissimilar areas and you will want to feather each mask separately. I do not recommend doing this on a single layer, because you want to apply effects like spill suppression and matte to isolated areas.

Once you have finished all of the separate keys, each with its own unique spill suppression, layer them on top of each other to create one master matte. The combined layers should be color-corrected as one unit.

I will explain the procedure step by step using Keylight in Adobe After Effects, but you could easily do this with any quality compositing tool, like Apple Shake, The Foundry Nuke, and even Apple Motion. The one "gotcha" is that you need a keyer that allows you to key "unpremultiplied." The ability to unpremultiply your result is crucial to a good key.

There are two types of alpha channels: straight and premultiplied. Straight, or unmatted, alpha channels have all of the transparency information in the alpha channel. Premultiplied alpha channels store the transparency information not only in the alpha but also a bit in the foreground. It takes a bit of your edge color from your foreground and brings it into the edge, with the purpose of smoothing your edges. This is great if the edges of the foreground plate match your background plate. If they do not match your background, they can cause an ugly fringe. In this case, when joining the alpha matte with the spill surpression, the results will multiply around the edges of your masks, giving you ugly thin dark lines. There is more on spill suppression in Chapter 16 under "Spill and despill."

Premultiplied gives you dark lines around the edge of your masks. By checking the Unpremultiplied Result box, you eliminate those lines. Footage courtesy of Angie Mistretta.

You do want your matte to be premultiplied eventually — *after* you color-correct.

The multiple edge mask technique in After Effects. This technique takes quite a bit of time but the results are stellar. I'm using The Foundry Keylight in this tutorial.

1. Drag your greenscreen footage into a new comp called *GMatte*. Garbage-matte the footage and take care of any preprocessing that needs to be done. Remember to feather your mask. Close the GMatte comp.

2. Drag the GMatte comp to the Create a New Composition button at the bottom of the Project window. A new comp will open, containing the GMatte precomp as a layer. Rename the layer *Core Matte*. Rename the comp *Final Key*. It is also helpful to change your background layer to a contrasting color, such as orange, so that you can see your any green fringe or cast that might be hiding around your edges.

3. Apply Keylight to your Core Matte layer. Adjust the settings so that you have a rough key and there are no holes in your matte. The edges do not need to be too accurate, since they'll be choked in. Adjust the Screen Pre-blur so that your matte tightens on your subject by about 10%. You should have smooth rounded edges on your matte without a lot of detail. Turn off the Core Matte while you work, so that you can focus on the layer at hand and toggle it on and off when needed to check blending.

4. Now it is time to isolate areas of your subject. Drag another copy of the GMatte comp into your Final Key comp and place it below your Core Matte in the timeline. Rename the layer as it corresponds to your footage (example: hair, arm, shirt — right). Use

Draw multiple masks on areas of different edge textures and colors.

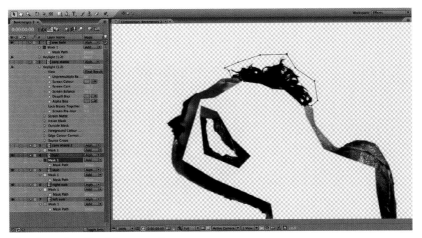

The edge matte without the core matte.

the Pen tool to isolate this area, using the bisection method as discussed in the section on making garbage mattes. Again, feather your mask. Always keep all edges soft so that they blend together. Apply Keylight, getting in as tightly and neatly as you can on the target area. Be diligent about checking for holes. If you have a spill, apply spill suppression. If you need a matte choker, apply it. Make the key as perfect as you possibly can, but *do not* color-correct your layer. Keep the Unpremultiply Result box checked. You don't want to see any matte lines in your composition!

5. Repeat Step 4 with each section of your actor, adjusting the matte choker and spill suppression as necessary for each section.

6. When all of your sections are finished, turn on your Core Matte layer and make sure that your layers overlap neatly throughout your timeline. Check for holes and fix any areas that aren't up to snuff.

7. Bring the Final Key comp into a new comp for compositing and color correction. This is also where you would add any light wrap.

Tip! If you need to make a Master Alpha Matte, drag the Final Key Comp to the Create a New Composition button. Apply Set Channels (Effect > Channel > Set Channels) to the Final Key layer. Set the Red, Green, and Blue source layers to Alpha. Your foreground image should be completely white now. This can be rendered out for several purposes and is good to have on hand.

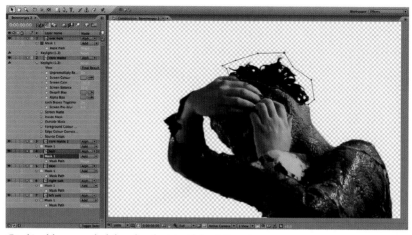

Combined layers masked, keyed and set to Alpha Add mode.

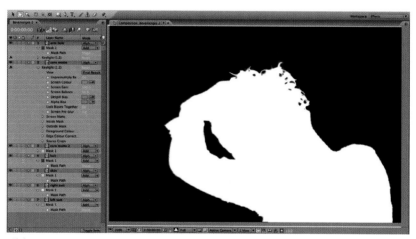

Alpha matte view.

For in-depth video training on this technique, check out Angie Mistretta's *Professional Keying with Keylight*, available at *Toolfarm.com*.

Automatically cycle mask colors in After Effects. Under After Effects > Preferences > User Interface Colors, check the Cycle Mask Colors so that each new mask doesn't default to yellow.

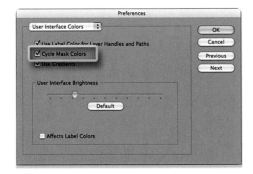

User Interface preferences in After Effects.

Color correction

Mismatched color temperature is a dead giveaway that your footage has been composited. If your background was shot outside, the light will be bluer, so make sure you give your foreground object a bluish color of lighting. If you're indoors, the color may be more orangey. You also want to remove any color cast on skin tones. With any color correction tool, brightness and contrast are a good place to start. It's important to match luminance between plates. You can get all scientific about matching shadow and highlight colors and levels, but I find that eyeballing usually takes care of most of the problem. I like to use Curves because you can adjust the blacks or whites without touching the midtones, and visa versa. Use Levels, Curves, and Hue/Saturation controls in your host application of choice to adjust the tonal range and shadows. Remember, you want it to look natural and believable.

Color correction in Apple Final Cut Pro. Final Cut Pro has some terrific three-way color correction tools that are very easy to use. Here are some Final Cut Pro color correction basics.

1. Select your clip in the timeline and apply the Color Corrector 3-way (Effects > Video Filters > Color Correcton > Color Corrector 3-way).
2. Double-click on your clip in the timeline to open the viewer.
3. Click on the tab in your viewer called Color Corrector 3-Way.

4. There are also waveform monitors and vectorscopes and more that allow you to view video levels, under Tools > Video Scopes.

5. Below the Mids in the Color Corrector 3-way are Auto Level and Match Hue controls, as well as a slider for saturation.

6. To change the color cast, click the eyedropper under Match Hue and select an area of white on your screen. This basically does a white balance for you.

7. Use the color wheels and sliders to tweak until you are happy with it.

Apple Final Cut Pro has very nice color correction tools. Footage courtesy of Douglas Toltzman, Oak Street Software.

Third-party options for color correction.

Red Giant Magic Bullet Colorista ($199) gives you Lift, Gamma, and Gain color wheels for easy adjustment of color balance and luminance. You can get very precise results with Colorista, and it has often brought my crummy dark footage back to life. Colorista is great for adjusting composites because it allows you to set highlight and shadow levels exactly and make flesh tones look natural. Colorista works in Adobe After Effects, Adobe Premiere Pro, Apple Final Cut Pro, Apple Motion, and Avid Xpress Pro/Media Composer.

Red Giant Magic Bullet Looks ($399) is my best cheat. In After Effects, if you apply Looks on an adjustment layer or on the entire precomposed or rendered movie, it automatically balances your color temperatures throughout your composition and gives you a beautiful filmic look. This is essentially a huge cheat, but man, is it easy — and just beautiful. Even if your keys and color temps look great across the board, I urge you to try Magic Bullet Looks on your footage. It's great for creating moods, mimicking film stocks, day for night, and for isolating areas of the shot you want to highlight. Looks also works in Adobe Premiere Pro, Apple Final Cut Pro, Apple Motion, and Avid Xpress Pro/Media Composer.

Red Giant Magic Bullet Looks ships with more than 100 incredible prebuilt Looks and everything is completely tweakable.

This is the Day for Night Look. I've added some Edge Softness to focus on the actor. 3D background courtesy of Paul Wood. Live footage courtesy of Angie Mistretta.

CHAPTER 16: FIXING PROBLEMS

Here are a few things that may give you some problems in your keying process.

- Hair and fur and other tough-to-key edges
- Removing tracking dots
- Bad spill
- Keying motion blur

Some of these can be fixed in post and others ... well, not so easily. Remember Rule No.4: We can't fix everything in post! There are tried-and-true methods and some innovative techniques to pull cleaner keys and make better composites no matter what problems you might encounter.

Hair and fur and other tough-to-key edges

Daniel Land, co-producer of *Dirty Trousers*, has an interesting tip for camouflaging and blending those tough-to-key edges: "There are little tricks that I've picked up over the years. I always leave a 1-2% transparency on the foreground layers; enough to allow some of the color/value to bleed through but not enough to notice." (You can do this by setting your foreground opacity to 98-99%.)

Matte tools. The Simple Choker in After Effects will shrink your matte one pixel at a time. It works really well for cleaning up that fringe on premultiplied alpha channels.

The Matte Choker in After Effects will smooth out and soften blocky edges, allowing you to get in tighter and blend more seamlessly into your background. It can be used to expand the edges to fill in holes as well.

Apple Motion also has a Matte Choker plug-in that ships with it in Final Cut Studio. Sometimes these tools just don't do enough, though.

Third-party matte tools. Of course, there's a plug-in to help with the time-consuming task of procedural mattes. Digital Film Tools Composite Suite ($295) for After Effects, Final Cut Pro, and Motion includes a plug-in called Composite. It has a great edge-blending feature that allows for color correction, blurring and mixing the edge to the background, and adding drop shadows. You can also modify the matte using Expand, Shrink, and Blur tools.

Red Giant has a couple of nice keying and matte tools. Key Correct Pro has been mentioned a few times and is invaluable when doing heavy-duty keying jobs. Key Correct Pro Alpha Cleaner kills grain and noise, fills in holes in the foreground, and fixes other challenging matte problems. You can cut out dark noise and sharpen matte edges with the Gamma Controls. It really lets you get a clean key around thin and soft edges, such as hair. The noise is removed but the detail remains.

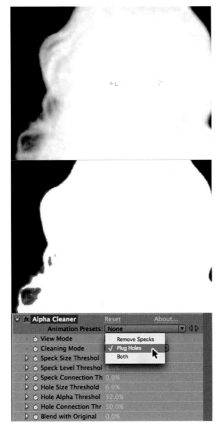

The top image is the original alpha channel. The Key Correct Pro Alpha Cleaner fixed alpha is just below it. Notice how the partially transparent areas in the hair and the specks in the eyes are fixed.

Key Correct Pro Alpha Blur helps soften chunky, blocky edges on your matte, and Key Correct Pro Matte Feather softens the edges of your alpha matte. Red Giant Software Composite Wizard ($299) will automate color correction effects, blur or feather your matte, and clean up unwanted artifacts. Then, of course, there is The Foundry Keylight, which has a most powerful and easy to use Matte Choker. You have lots of options.

Removing tracking dots

Tracking dots are those marks on the greenscreen used to accurately position the digital environments behind the actors for any of the moving camera shots in the greenscreen environments. They need to be removed from your scene. You could mask them out but you can also paint on the alpha channel to remove them in After Effects. This is a very fast method if your clip is short; otherwise you'll spend a lot of time painting out dots.

1. Set your Workspace to Paint. The pull-down menu is in the upper right corner of After Effects and this puts your Paint tools right on screen for you. The Paint tool will be in the upper right corner and Brush Tips directly below.

2. Double-click your foreground layer so that the Layer window opens. You can only paint in the Layer window.

3. We want to paint the stray tracking dots out of the alpha channel, so choose Channels: Alpha in the Paint window. Set the Duration to Single Frame if your actor passes in front of the tracking dot. If the shot is locked down and the actor does not cross in front of the dot, you can choose Constant.

4. Choose the size of brush tip you would like to use. It should be about the size of the dots you need to remove.

5. Click on the Layer window and paint out the tracking dots. Go frame by frame by tapping the Page Down key (or Page Up to go backward) and paint out the dots. A Paint effect is added to your Effect Controls window.

Paint out tracking dots with the Paint tool in After Effects.

Of course, this technique can be used for much more than just painting out tracking dots. You can clean up dust and holes in alphas and much more when you use the Paint and Clone tools on your footage.

Spill and despill

Several keyers have built-in spill suppression, several of which have been mentioned previously. What exactly is spill? Well, to expand on what we covered earlier in the book, it's the leaked green that is reflected onto the actor from the greenscreen. It can show up in light-colored clothing, around the edge of skin and hair, and on shiny and reflective items. Spill is a problem that you definitely need to take care of for a believable key.

Spill suppression in After Effects

1. Apply a Spill Suppressor (Effect > Keying > Spill Suppressor) to the footage with green.
2. Choose the Color to suppress. You might have to zoom in to the edge to grab some green with the eyedropper tool.
3. Adjust the amount of suppression.

Another option in After Effects is to use the Channel Mixer effect (Effects > Color Correction > Channel Mixer). Adjust the Red-Green and Blue-Green settings. This works best for shots with just a little bit of spill. You can also try adjusting Hue/Saturation (Effects > Color Correction > Hue/Saturation in After Effects). Choose Greens from the Channel Control and turn down the green saturation. If you still have some spill, adjust the Channel Range of the Yellows and Cyans, green's neighbors.

Third-party options for spill suppression. Red Giant Software Key Correct Pro Spill Killer removes green spill that shows up in your image. In my opinion, this works better than the After Effects Spill Suppressor. The Foundry Keylight, Red Giant Primatte Keyer Pro, and Digital Film Tools zMatte all have built-in spill suppressors, which were covered in Chapter 14.

The image on the left has bad spill. The image on the right has Red Giant Key Correct Pro Spill Killer applied. Footage courtesy of Daniel Land, Unit Circle Films.

Keying motion-blurred footage

Blurred footage is very difficult to key and you usually end up losing fingers in the process, so hopefully you have shot with a higher shutter speed to help eliminate the blur. The downside to this is that your footage doesn't always look as natural without the motion blur.

So can you fix it? Well ... good luck. It's highly likely that there is absolutely nothing you can do about it. At least it's quick, so your viewers may not even notice. You can try to isolate the area of the fast-moving item and then tint it. In the shot used in the Spill Killer example, the man in the middle hands a newspaper to the man in the front. The movement is so fast that the newspaper disappears when it is keyed. By isolating the object and tinting it before it is keyed, you may be able to rescue it.

Another potential solution is to duplicate your keyed layer and use a mask to isolate the area that is blurred out. You will need to dilate the Matte Choke and check to make sure that your keyer and pre-process effects, such as a Smooth Screen effect, aren't eating away at the edges of the blurred area too much. Use a blend mode such as Darken on the duplicated area, feather your mask, and adjust the opacity of the layer until it blends. This probably won't completely fix the problem but it may improve things somewhat.

Third-party options for keying motion-blurred footage. There are some third-party plug-ins to help key shots with bad motion blur, such as dvMatte Pro from dvGarage.

CHAPTER 17: MAKING YOUR COMPOSITE LOOK BELIEVABLE

Now that you have a good grasp on keying and all of the work that goes into it, I'm going to let you in on a secret. The key to a believable composite is to match the background and foreground plates. It's not about pulling a perfect key. There are a lot of things to think about when making a great composite: highlights, light angle, reflections, flipping shots, light wrap, and matching grain. Here are some methods of getting the best match you can.

Matching grain

When your foreground and background plates come from different sources, it's very important to match the grain. You will need to match the grain between different stocks of footage, footage shot on different cameras, and footage with different lighting. Photos will not have moving grain, and 3D is often so clean that it needs a bit of grain to make it look less pristine. Also, if you've blurred and scaled your video, the grain structure is changed and you may need to add more grain.

Matching grain in After Effects. Adobe After Effects has a very nice Remove Grain filter, which was covered in Chapter 12, and an equally nice tool to do the opposite: the Match Grain tool.

1. Apply Match Grain to less grainy footage or your 3D or image file, since they will have little or no grain (Effects > Noise & Grain > Match Grain).
2. Choose the Noise Source layer, which will probably be your keyed layer.
3. Adjust your Preview Region, which works just like the Remove Grain plug-in.

4. Tweak the intensity, size, and other parameters until it looks good to you.

There is also an Add Grain filter (Effects > Noise & Grain > Add Grain), which is set up in a similar manner.

Light **wrap**

A light wrap, in the simplest sense, is just a splash of light that is reflected on the edges of your foreground plate from your background plate. It usually reflects the colors and luminance levels of your background layer and will make your composite look more natural.

The easiest way to do this is with a plug-in. Several keying plug-ins include a light wrap function, such as Red Giant's Primatte Keyer Pro. Red Giant's Key Correct Pro has a separate tool for light wrap that allows you to choose your background layer and does the work for you.

You can create a light wrap without a plug-in but it takes some time and a bit of patience and can be easy to screw up. My friend Matt Schirado showed me his technique for building a light wrap from scratch. This is a modified version, using After Effects.

1. In After Effects, bring your greenscreen footage and your background layer into a new composition. Name the composition Light Wrap Final.

2. Apply your keying plug-in to your foreground plate and key as necessary. A composition that has been previously keyed using the multiple mask method could also be used here.

3. Select your keyed foreground plate. Duplicate it twice so that you have three copies in your composition (Command + D/Ctrl + D).

4. Select and duplicate your background plate so that you have two copies in your composition. The light wrap final composition should now contain five layers.

5. Select one layer of your background and two of your foreground layers. You will want to nest these into their own composition. Go to Layer > Precompose in your menu.

    A dialog box will open. Rename your new composition Light Wrap and make sure the box that says Open New Composition is checked.

Precompose two copies of your foreground plate and one copy of your background plate.

6. In the Light Wrap comp, let's first set up the layers and their modes.

   Background layer: Place at the bottom layer. Set the TrkMat to Alpha. Your background should now appear through the keyhole created by your footage, but you may not see this because you have two layers of your foreground above it. Feel free to toggle the visibility of the top layer.

   Center layer: This is a keyed footage layer. As soon as you changed the background layer to Alpha, this layer's visibility should have turned off. The background layer is using this layer as a keyhole. Note: You will only see the effect if you turn off the top layer.

   Top layer: This is a keyed footage layer and make sure that the visibility is turned on. Set the mode to Stencil Alpha.

7. On the top layer, layer 1, apply Minimax (Effect > Channel > Minimax). Set the Operation to Minimum, Radius to 2 or 3, and the Channel to Alpha and Color. Make sure you tick the box "Don't Shrink Edges." Your matte should be slightly smaller.

   Apply Invert to the same top footage layer (Effect > Channel > Invert). You should now see an outline in the shape of your keyed footage, with the background coming through.

   Apply Fast Blur to the same top layer (Effect > Blur & Sharpen > Fast Blur). Set the blurriness fairly high; I set my blurriness to 48.

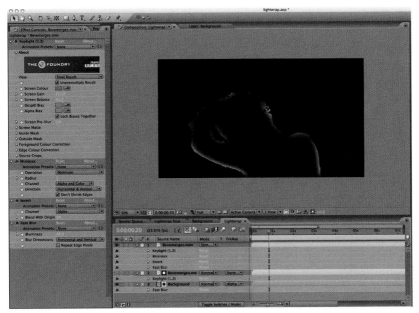

The order of effects and the order of layers are of the utmost importance when building your own light wrap. One small mistake can throw everything in the entire light wrap off. This image demonstrates the correct settings.

Leave the Blur dimensions set to Horizontal and Vertical, and check the Repeat Edge Pixels box.

8. On your bottom layer, the background layer, apply a Fast Blur. Use the same settings as above, but adjust your blurriness as needed. You do not want to see any detail from your background, just the blurred light and color.

9. Close the Light Wrap composition and open Light Wrap Final. You should have three layers in the Light Wrap Final composition:
    *   Light Wrap comp: Layer 1 (top layer)
    *   Keyed Footage: Layer 2 (center layer)
    *   Background: Layer 3 (bottom layer)

    Set the mode of the Light Wrap layer to Screen or Add or Lighten. See which works best for your footage. If you need to make it brighter, apply Levels. You will also probably want to turn down the opacity of the layer. Make sure your edges don't appear to be see-through.

There you have it — building your own light wrap from scratch. Not difficult, but a lot of steps. If you can afford it, get a plug-in.

The top image has no light wrap. The bottom image has the light wrap applied.

There are several third-party plug-ins that are made for light wrapping, including Red Giant Software Key Correct Pro and Primatte Keyer Pro, The Foundry Keylight, and Digital Film Tools zMatte. I prefer to use a plug-in because it's much faster and involves a lot less messing.

Light angle

"Matching the angle of sunlight with the studio lights is crucial, as is the shot framing," says Daniel Land, co-producer of *Dirty Trousers*. Daniel and his crew use printouts of the background plates to match lighting angles while shooting in the greenscreen studio.

Jonas Hummelstrand of *GeneralSpecialist.com* adds, "You can fix almost anything in postproduction, but relighting is among the hardest and least successful things you want to spend your nights with. There's nothing that screams fake as much as wrong lighting!"

What if you didn't get it right on the shoot? Viewers of your film may not even notice the differing light angles specifically, but they will definitely feel something is "not quite right" with the composite. How do you fix it? If you have a completely opposite angle, you can try flipping your background or your actor, if the scene will allow for it.

Worst-case scenario, you can dim the highlights and brighten up the shadows using curves or levels to camouflage the problem.

Depth of field

The Depth of field rule of thumb:

- Wide shot: Your foreground object/actor and background will have the same focus, with possibly some depth of field effect on far-off scenery.
- Medium shot: Your actor will be in focus and your background will have some defocus.
- Close-up: Your actor will be in focus and your background will be more defocused.

There are a number of defocus and blur tools that are included with most host applications and a multitude of third-party options.

The close-up has a more defocused background. The medium shot has a slightly defocused back-ground. The wide shot has a slight depth of field blur, way off in the distance. Footage courtesy of Angie Mistretta. Backgrounds courtesy of iStockPhoto. 3D image courtesy of Paul Wood.

Reintroducing reflections

Many times you'll want to replace a greenscreened area with a window glass or other reflective surface. An obvious example is when you are shooting a car on a greenscreen. You will want to add environmental reflections. Duplicating your background footage, masking off areas, flipping it if necessary, and using layer modes will quite often give you a good result.

One trick for shiny surfaces such as cars and windows that are in an outdoor environment is to reflect some clouds on them. This can be done with Fractal Noise in After Effects (Effects > Noise > Fractal Noise) or a cloud-generating filter, or even with some stock footage of moving clouds. Layer the clouds over the object and turn the opacity down very, very low. A blend mode also helps and you will want to mask and feather the edges of your cloud layer so they don't show. The key is to be subtle. You don't want the audience to notice the clouds, but you want to give your world a bit of realism and texture. For a bit more pizzazz, apply subtle lens flares where light would hit the object.

The composite with no added reflections. Footage courtesy of iStockPhoto.com.

The windshield and dash-board have sky color and clouds reflected on them. The effect here is not all that subtle. Footage courtesy of iStockPhoto.com.

If you have dull-looking footage, you can brighten the current high-lights by adjusting the levels and curves. You can also duplicate your layer, add a slight blur to the top layer, and then use a Blend mode on the top layer to blend the layers together. Adjust opacity to taste. This technique can also help soften harshness and works to dim overly bright areas when you set the Blend mode to Darken or Multiply.

Light effects were added to this shot with Red Giant Magic Bullet Looks. Foreground footage courtesy of Angie Mistretta. Back-ground footage from iStockPhoto.com.

Creating shadows

Shadows have their own color, darkness, and blur characteristics, something that's important to keep in mind when you're creating your own shadows. In After Effects, I have a technique for making my foreground object have a drop shadow, because the built-in Drop Shadow plug-in just doesn't cut it for a look like this. You need to accurately project an object shadow onto a surface, not just create a dark spot behind it. This technique works best when you have the full actor or object on your screen.

1. Duplicate your foreground object and rename it Shadow.
2. Drag the Shadow layer below your object.
3. Make the Shadow layer 3D by clicking the little isometric square in the timeline.
4. Move the anchor point to the base/feet of the actor. This will be the point where a natural shadow would come from the actor.

Adjust the angle of the shadow by making the layer 3D and then using the Rotate tools to position it to match the other shadows. 3D courtesy of Paul Wood.

5. Use the Rotate tools to rotate the shadow so that it matches the angle of the shadows in your background.

6. Fill the shadow with an appropriate shadow color (Effect > Generate > Fill).

7. Add a blur such as Fast Blur (Effects > Blur & Sharpen > Fast Blur).

8. You may want to try using Blend modes but you want to be careful not to multiply shadows on top of each other.

This could also be done by making the foreground and background plates 3D layers, adding some lights from an angle, and having the background accept shadows. The first method is easier to set up and control, but you can get some nice shadow effects by having a layer cast shadows but not accept lights, since you probably do not want to alter your lighting.

Third-party solutions for projecting shadows. Red Giant Software Image Lounge ($299) has a very handy filter called Real Shadows that can accurately project a shadow onto a surface.

Red Giant Warp ($199) contains three powerful plug-ins to give you ultimate control over shadows, reflections, and corner point warps. The Shadow tool renders realistic shadows for text or subjects shot on greenscreen.

Adding motion blur back into the video

Daniel Land, co-producer of *Dirty Trousers*, says, "We kept the shutter at 1/60 for the most part, but there were certainly deviations from that from time to time. In general we just had to be aware of motion blur in the action sequences."

If you shot with a high shutter speed to eliminate motion blur and make your key smoother, that was a smart move. Adding some blur back into the motion will make the movements look more natural. If you use the Motion Blur filter, it will apply the effect to your entire plate. You can get creative with masking and layering, or you can use a plug-in such as RE:Vision Effects ReelSmart Motion Blur ($149.95).

"Add motion blur in post by using optical flow technologies such as ReelSmart Motion Blur, and add depth of field by layering chroma clips and post-blurring them," says Jonas Hummelstrand on his terrific motion graphics blog, *GeneralSpecialist.com*. ReelSmart Motion Blur is available for Adobe After Effects, Adobe Premiere Pro, Autodesk Combustion, and Apple Final Cut Pro. OFX, Nuke, and Toxik versions are also available, plus it supports 32-bit float point color space in After Effects.

CHAPTER 18: COOL TRICKS AND INSPIRATION

This chapter is designed to give you the postproduction conclusion to some of the production scenarios we covered on pages 51-53, which should give you expanded ideas of when to use your newfound keying knowledge, as well as when you should not use keying. These ideas come from personal work experience, conversations with visual effects artists, and even some behind-the-scenes articles about keying and visual effects.

Dancing clothes, aka the invisible man

I used to work at a video post house called Postworks. We had a very cool job come in for a chain of outlet malls in which the client wanted to show bodiless clothes dancing around over a white screen of infinite nothingness.

The costume designer bought special Lycra/spandex-type fabric and made bodysuits that covered the hands and feet fully. These were skintight and in the bluest shade of blue in existence. There were also hoods made to cover the face and hair of the models. The models put on the bodysuits with the season's hottest fashions on top and danced in front of a bluescreen.

The footage was brought into the editor and keyed. The one problem was the inside of the collars, which had to be tracked and rotoscoped back in.

Red lips, gray face

The look used in *Sin City* and other films, where there is one primary color and the rest of the footage is completely desaturated, can be easily pulled off by using green makeup or a bright green item of clothing. For example, if you want only the lips of a woman to be red and the rest of the shot black-and-white, have the actor put on the sickest shade of bright green non-glossy lipstick you can find. Creating the effect is easy.

1. Bring the footage into your host application's timeline.
2. Duplicate the footage. On the bottom layer, use Hue/Saturation or a similar filter to remove any color from the shot. Toggle the visibility of the top layer to see the effect.
3. On the top layer, use your keyer to key out the green lips, then invert the alpha matte.
4. Color-correct or tint the lips any shade that you need and adjust your matte as needed.

Key smoke and fire? Not! or How to remove a black background from fire, explosions, smoke, window cracks, etc.

Instead of keying out the black you'll get a much nicer effect by using Blend modes. If you're shooting fire or smoke, shoot it over black. In your timeline, in the Modes area, set the Layer mode for your footage to Add, Screen, or Lighten, depending on what looks the best.

Original Window Crack Image has the layer mode set to Screen to remove black.

The Blend mode settings in After Effects can give you some great options for compositing. Images from iStockPhoto.com.

For the cracked windshield in the example, I used Screen mode. To give it more depth, I duplicated the layer, Inverted it (Effect > Channel > Invert and use default settings), and then set the mode to Multiply. I nudged the position of the layer over and down by one pixel and made sure this darker layer was below the lighter layer.

Blend modes are a fast way to remove the black background from window cracks, smoke, fire, and explosions. Images from iStockPhoto.com.

Replace television or computer screens

Have you ever tried to shoot a computer monitor on video? Unless everything is set up perfectly, the screen will roll. You might think that the easiest way to replace a screen would be to put a solid green background image up on the television or computer screen, key it, and replace it with non-rolling content, right? Wrong.

Leave your monitor off while you shoot it, so you'll get all of those natural reflections that you'd miss with a bright green screen.

1. In After Effects, create a solid and mask it to the exact size of your screen. Track and corner pin the footage if it is a moving shot so that the solid will follow and cover the screen you want to replace.

2. Add your replacement video to the composition, and scale and position as needed.

3. If it is a moving shot that you had to track, parent your replacement video to the solid that you cut out.

4. Duplicate your original screen shot and the solid. Use the solid as an alpha matte for the original screen shot. Use a Blend mode such as Lighten, Screen, or Add to bring the highlights back to the screen, then adjust the opacity.

CHAPTER 19: THE *SIN CITY* CONUNDRUM: BLENDING 3D BACKGROUNDS WITH KEYED FOOTAGE

Greenscreen footage courtesy of Angie Mistretta. Background adapted from original scene made by Ralph Caldwell and rendered by Toby Gaines. Reprinted with permission of MicroFilmmaker Magazine.

We've all seen it. The silky smooth combination of live action and rendered backgrounds that made us thrill to movies like *Sin City*. While we can all recall bad renditions from the past, nothing thrills us so much as seeing it done right. *The 300* also came to life because of the fusion of clean greenscreening and Lightwave backgrounds. How do you combine the artificial with the realistic and not end up with something that looks fake?

Well, this is largely determined by a combination of three elements: your choice of 3D software, the similarity of the lighting, and your attention to details.

Choosing a 3D software that meets your needs

Choosing the right 3D software for your needs involves knowing both how often you want to combine 3D backgrounds with your composites and what you can afford. The two are related: The more 3D work you're going to want to do, the more money you're going to want to save to get something that makes doing it easier. Although 3D definitely gives you the most creative options, many realistic composites with very effective backgrounds can be achieved by cutting out elements from high-resolution photos of exotic locales and pasting them into After Effects in a pseudo-3D format. And if you have the CS3 (or above) packages of both Photoshop and After Effects, you can create very realistic 3D buildings and interiors from photographs using Photoshop's enhanced Vanishing Point features, and then rotate them in After Effects. The cost of some of the software we're going to discuss below can be a bit off-putting, so consider checking out these alternative options.

Obviously, I can't go into all the 3D packages out there. Instead, I've focused on the three that I have the most experience with and that fit best with the parameters of this book.

Credits: Cinema 4D: Original scene created by Ralph Caldwell; Vue: Scene adapted and rendered by Sam Fisher; Lightwave: Scene adapted and rendered by Toby Gaines. Reprinted with permission of MicroFilmmaker Magazine.

In filmmaking, people talk about the pyramid of Fast, Cheap, and Good. You can only pick two. If you want a Fast and Cheap movie, it won't be Good. If you want a Fast and Good movie, it won't be Cheap. Well, 3D software selection seems to have a similar pyramid: Price, Power, and Ease of Use. If you want something that's comparatively inexpensive and powerful, it's not going to be terribly easy to use. A great example of this is Lightwave ($900), which is one of the most robust modeling and rendering packages under $1,000 on the market but has a very steep learning curve. Likewise, if you want software that's easy to use and powerful, it won't be terribly cheap. Maxon's Cinema 4D ($900 to $3,500) is a personal favorite because it's powerful and easy to use, but to get the most realistic render-ings you have to jump from their $900 package to their $2,200-to-$3,500 packages. (Maxon's president has, however, indicated their intention to include the photorealistic rendering options needed for greenscreen backgrounds in their basic 3D package in the future. They also have future plans for including an environmental creator specifically for greenscreen use in their low-end package.)

It's extremely worthwhile to download demos for both Lightwave and Cinema 4D to see how they would fit your needs. I also recommend looking at Vue ($140 to $900). Their Infinite package, at about $700, is worth checking out. It's specially designed for creating outdoor/fantasy environments — including clouds, forests, lakes, islands, mountains, and the like — and has become a big tool in Industrial Light and Magic's chest, most recently creating natural environments in *Pirates of the Caribean: Dead Man's Chest* and *The Spiderwick Chronicles*. Infinite isn't just about the outdoors, though; it has a decent toolbox of abilities for rendering indoor environments as well, along with a number of powerful pre-sets. The overall learning curve isn't too bad until you get into more serious tweaking, which can become a bit overwhelming for the newcomer. Luckily, there are a few Vue training books on the market. Best of all for low-budget filmmakers is that they have a completely functional learning edition, which you can download for free. The learning edition will let you render Standard-Definition movies and backgrounds without a watermark for a month. After that, it will put a watermark on everything, but it won't disable the program, so you can take some time to really see what Vue is capable of before you shell out any cash for it. A small warning: While Vue is quite powerful, it is the slowest-rendering of the three programs I've mentioned, which can be frustrating if you're rendering out animated backgrounds.

Pre-created 3D scenes designed for programs like Adobe Ultra can give a lot of 3D power to filmmakers who don't want to have to create the scenes themselves. Picture printed with permission of Adobe, Inc.

Creating **3D backgrounds in 3D software**

The screen shots on page 134 are from Cinema 4D, but the principles are pretty universal for all 3D programs for compositing.

First, to the best of your ability, you want to match the lens of your "virtual" camera as closely as you can to the lens of the camera with which you actually have shot or will shoot your greenscreen footage. (Creating original backgrounds in a 3D program is the one area where you can get away with generating a background *after* you've shot your footage; this can give you a lot of flexibility when you're shooting, so long as you don't get beyond your capabilities as a 3D artist during production.) While the match doesn't have to be exact, the closer you can come, the better the blend of your footage will appear. If your footage is already shot and you didn't write down the zoom/lens settings, cameras like Panasonic's HVX200A will generate metadata that you can check in metadata viewing software like Adobe's Bridge.

You also want to match the lighting in your scene with the angle and color of the lighting on your actors. If you haven't yet shot your greenscreen footage, seriously think through the lighting to make sure it replicates the lighting you set up in the 3D scene. Obviously, if a rendered scene requires five lights from five angles and you only have four lights to work with, you pretty much need to get rid of one of those lights in your 3D scene. Sometimes you can use a bounce card to simulate an extra light, but it's best not to rely on this sort of cheat because it can only replicate a fairly weak light source.

Rendering **your backgrounds correctly**

When it comes time to render the background, remember what your final output size is designed to be. If you don't want to do post movement on your background, render it to be the correct size and aspect ratio for your needs. If you want to add some creative movement, consider rendering a higher-resolution image that you can pan or tilt across. This can be a great way to cheat realism in post. Tilting from a starry sky to a couple looking at the stars, for example, can really sell the illusion of a wide, open environment.

Afterward, make sure that you retain vital 3D information, which can be utilized in applications like After Effects, Motion, and Shake. There are a couple of different ways to do this.

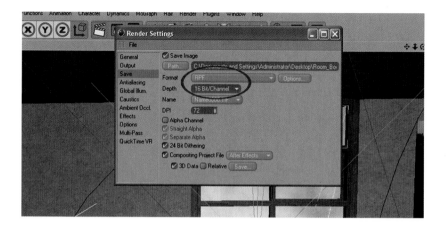

One of the most universal ways is to render and save images as either .rpf or .rla format images. These images are designed to store things like Z-depth, material information, and camera information so that you can precisely composite 3D backgrounds with your greenscreen footage. Unfortunately, this isn't a moving format like QuickTime or AVI, so if you're going to be creating an animated background, you'll have to create separate RPF/RLA images in a sequence.

Multipass exports can give you access to a variety of different elements, from depth maps to lighting maps.

If you want to have more power and control — and the ability to export actual movies — a lot of 3D programs export their information in such a way that they can be opened directly by a specific effects compositing software package like Shake or After Effects. For example, if you're using Cinema 4D R9 and above (or Carrara Pro 5 and above) and you want to do your final composite in After Effects, you can generate a .AEC file. This will allow After Effects to import your picture information — and 3D information — as a full AE project. (To be able to open and interact with .AEC files, you have to install the .AEC Exchange plug-in from Maxon's Web site into your After Effects Plug-in directory.) You need to make sure that you render out your information as a MultiPass picture or QuickTime in conjunction with saving a .AEC file, because the MultiPass file will contain most of the content information that the .AEC will reference. (Think of the .AEC as the actual After Effects composition and the MultiPass file as the asset files you will need.)

Once different elements are exported from your 3D application in the appropriate manner, many of the elements can be manipulated in After Effects or Motion.

Because these multipass files contain all your assets, they can be quite large, with single MultiPass images being 500 or more megabytes and short movies being many gigabytes, depending on the length of the animation, the complexity of the scene, and the number of 3D features exported. For Cinema 4D users, there are additional preset encoding formats besides the one for After Effects, thus allowing you to export similar files for Shake, Motion, Combustion, and Digital Fusion, as well.

3D channel effects in After Effects

Those 3D channel effects in Adobe After Effects that you may have tried to use but couldn't get to do anything? Well, they do something quite amazing once you know how they work.

Depth matte effect: placing your greenscreen shot within your 3D environment. With a normal .tiff or .jpeg file or QuickTime movie rendered in your 3D application, there is no way to actually place your 3D object between elements of your 3D composite. With the magic of .rpf files and the Depth Matte 3D Channel effect in After Effects, you can!

1. Bring your .rpf file into After Effects, just as you would any file: File > Import > find your file.
2. Drag the .rpf file into a new or existing composition.
3. Apply Depth Matte to the .rpf file layer: Effects > 3D Channel > Depth Matte.
4. Adjust the value of the Depth setting until you see only the portion you want in front of your actor.
5. Place your actor in the scene behind the object.
6. Duplicate your .rpf layer (Command + D/Ctrl + D) and make sure it's on the layer behind your actor.

The Depth Matte 3D Channel effect in After Effects. 3D Courtesy of Paul Wood.

7. On the Depth Matte options, check the Invert box. If you see a sharp edge, adjust the Depth on the layer behind your actor.

8. On the layer in front of your actor, adjust the Feather.

Depth of field with .rpf files. The Depth of Field 3D Channel effect simulates the camera's depth of field. It allows you to adjust the focus of a layer in areas that you determine by referencing the depth information in the .rpf file. You can blur the background and keep the foreground in focus to draw the viewer's attention to a certain area. See Chapter 17 for specifics on realistic depth of field settings.

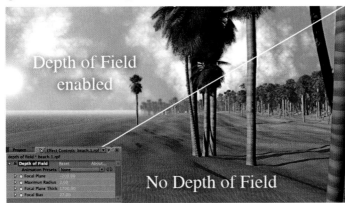

Depth of Field 3D Channel effect with .rpf file. 3D file courtesy of Paul Wood.

To give your .rpf file depth of field:

1. Import your .rpf into After Effects and add it to a comp. Apply the Depth of Field filter (Effects > 3D Channel > Depth of Field). Nothing will happen at first.

2. Adjust the Maximum Radius. This is the amount of blur. Keep it very low, just 1 or 2, to keep it realistic. The setting is a bit sensitive.

3. Find out how large your Focal Plane Thickness is by measuring the Z-depth in your image. View the Info window and then click in your composition and find the farthest point and the closest point. Subtract the smaller value from the larger value and this is your Focal Plane.

4. Focal Bias makes the adjustments more sensitive. Use a lower number for more preciseness.

5. Finally, Focal Plane determines where the blur is located, and can be keyframed if you want to simulate a rack focus.

Depth info.

```
Info ×
    R : 92        X : 1296
    G : 86      + Y : 520
    B : 42
    A : 255
Layer Coordinates: 1236, 524
Depth −1661.49
```

Matching your 3D and footage

Much of the time, 3D looks much too clean and adding some grain will help match it to your footage. Adding Grain is covered in Chapter 17. You also need to add a very small amount of blur to your 3D to match the focus of your footage, but a depth of field effect may be a better solution. Matching shadows and highlights, light angles, and all those other important tasks that were also discussed in the chapter are all crucial to a good composite.

CHAPTER 20: THE FUTURE OF LOW-BUDGET KEYING

At 2008's NAB, the potential future of low-budget keying was announced: the RED Scarlet 3K. Designed to bring high-quality color recording to lower-budget filmmakers, the RED Scarlet marks the first time that low-budget filmmakers can have nearly Hollywood-quality tools for their greenscreen creations. From Oakley founder Jim Jannard's start-up company RED, the camera is slated to be released sometime in the next year or two and aims to boast a 3K resolution in RAW format for a targeted price point of just $3,000. (At the time of this printing, that's less than the cost of a Panasonic SD DVX100B and nearly half the cost of the Panasonic HD HVX200A.)

This RAW format, which is used by most DSLR still cameras, retains virtually all image choices except zoom and depth of field as nondestructive information. This means that a lot of high-quality color correcting can be done in post, but most important to us is that it means the 4:4:4 color space we discussed in Chapter 1 is retained. Additionally, because the 3K resolution is 160% the size of 1080P, you can key your footage at a higher resolution

The beta model of the RED Scarlet 3K shown at a recent trade show.

and then shrink it down to the size you need. These two factors should yield much, much cleaner keys than have ever been possible for low-budget filmmakers to achieve before. To give you an idea of just how large 3K really is, most digital projection theaters still only have 2K projectors, which means that low-budget filmmakers could essentially be capable of better than theater-quality productions in the near future. (Immediately before publication, a redesign on the Scarlet was announced by RED, "due to changes in the industry." The changes mentioned likely refer to stiff competition from other companies like Nikon and Canon, who are wading into the high-quality video market at a similar price point. For more developments on this, as well as news about other improvements for low-budget filmmakers, be sure to check out the latest updates at: *http://www.microfilmmaker.com*.)

Of course, cameras are not the only way in which the future of low-budget greenscreen creation is improving. Even as this book was being written, new improvements were being unveiled by countless software companies around the world. While the actual keying software continues to slowly improve as software packages are augmented by more powerful algorithms for dealing with highly compressed footage, programs designed for creating environments grow more powerful and useful as well. We mentioned in Chapter 19, "The *Sin City* Conundrum," that new 3D companies were planning on unveiling revolutionary ways to create 3D environments for low-budget filmmakers in the near future.

Well, shortly before publication, Maxon released Cinema 4D R11, which features a new creation engine called "Projection Man." Prior to its release as part of R11, "Projection Man" had been a secret project that Maxon had created for Hollywood studios, enabling those studios to create realistic backgrounds for movies like *Spider-Man 3*, *Beowulf*, and many others. Somewhat like a more advanced version of the improved Vanishing Point rolled out in Adobe Photoshop CS3, this engine allows photo-realistic backgrounds to be mapped to simple primitive shapes inside Cinema 4D. (Unlike Photoshop, the textures can be mapped to curved and oblong surfaces.) This essentially enables you to create powerful, believable 3D models and environments in a fraction of the time that would have been possible before.

As you can see, the technology for greenscreen production and post-production continues to grow and improve with each passing year, making the capacity of the low-budget filmmaker to suspend the disbelief of the viewer greater than it's ever been before.

CONCLUSION

Greenscreen and keying can open your film up to endless possibilities. Want to create a scene on a mountaintop but you're shooting in Indiana? No problem! How about a scene on Mars or aboard a UFO? Why not! You're no longer limited by your physical location. What can limit you, however, is lack of patience and time. Keying takes practice, practice, practice and lots of trial and error. Learn the basics and get comfortable with the tools and you could create the next big indie film.

That said, there is so much more to filmmaking than the special effects. A good narrative is priceless, not to mention things like talented actors

The final composite with greenscreen footage, an .rpf file of the beach, some 3D Channel effects in After Effects and treated with Magic Bullet Looks.

with interesting characters, continuity, set design and costumes, cinematography, and editing. Oh, there is so much to worry about!

I was watching *At the Earth's Core*, a 1976 sci-fi/fantasy film that epitomizes the term "B" movie. The film is an adaptation of the Edgar Rice Burroughs book about a Victorian era scientist and his financier who take an earth-boring machine on a test through a mountain. They end up in a strange land at the center of the earth, complete with telepathic dinosaur-bird creatures controlled by aliens and, of course, a beautiful woman to rescue. The low-budget effects were incredibly fake-looking and corny but the story is bizarre, fun, and filled with action (and a lot of bad science!). It was mesmerizing. Maybe it was the telepathic dinosaur-birds controlling my mind!

By comparison, I caught the two newest *Star Wars* movies on cable around the same time. These *Star Wars* flicks cost millions with their incredible visual effects, and they have mind-blowingly cool-looking 3D environments, beautiful compositing between the 3D and keyed actors, and realistic explosions. Yes, the films are a spectacle, but they lack the heart of the first three *Star Wars* films, which completely won me over. I really didn't care about Anakin's spiral to the dark side or the fate of Padme and her unborn twins. The plots seemed to get more convoluted as the trilogy progressed and there were (literally) an army of characters that I couldn't keep straight. *The Empire Strikes Back* they are not. I'll admit it, I cried when Han Solo was frozen in carbonite.

I will freely admit that I preferred *At the Earth's Core* over *Revenge of the Sith* because of the compelling story, not the effects. Chances are, your budgets are nowhere near what George Lucas or Stephen Spielberg has to spend on effects (who has that kind of money?!). The lesson here is that you do not need a huge budget and over-the-top effects for a good film. Character-driven stories with strong dialogue and a solid plot will take you far. On the other side of the argument, great effects and compositing can make or break your film, especially with today's audiences who expect stellar visual effects. Films like *Titanic* and *The Lord of the Rings* have upped the ante, even for the low-budget filmmaker, and there is no going back to 1976. Basically, you need it all. Hopefully this book will help you achieve some high-quality visual effects and give your low-budget film a high-budget look. (Hint: Throw on some Magic Bullet Looks! It can be our secret.) The good script is up to you.

RESOURCE LIST

Lighting and shooting and greenscreen equipment

Most hardware items can be found at B&H: BHPhotoVideo.com or from the vendors' Web sites.

Apollo Softbox: *BHPhotoVideo.com*
Chimera: *chimeralighting.com*
Divergent Media ScopeBox: *ScopeBox.com*
Elsdon Enterprises FX (EEFX): *eefx.com*
Fresnel lenses: *BHPhotoVideo.com*
ImageWest Lighting: *imagewest.tv*
Lee Filters: *leefilters.com*
Lowel lighting equipment: lowel.com
Nikon: *nikon.com*
Olympic/CCA Botanical Green paint: *Lowes.com*
Panasonic HVX200A Camera: *panasonic.com*
Photoflex CineDome Softbox: *photoflex.com*
RED camera: *RED.com*
Real Stream Adaptor: *BHPhotoVideo.com*
Reflecmedia Chromatte / LiteRing: *reflecmedia.com*
Rosco Paint/ DigiComp: *Rosco.com*
Smith Victor lights: *smithvictor.com*
Sony: *Sony.com*
Zylight: *zylight.com*

Video Plug-ins, Software, etc.

Most video plug-ins and software mentioned in this book are available at *Toolfarm.com* or the vendors' Web sites.

Adobe After Effects, Photoshop, OnLocation, Ultra: *Adobe.com*
Apple Final Cut Studio, Shake: *Apple.com*
Artbeats Stock Footage: *Artbeats.com*
Autodesk 3ds Max: *Autodesk.com*
Boris FX, Inc. Continuum Complete: *Borisfx.com*
CHV Bezier Garbage Matte Pro: *Chv-plugins.com*
Daz Carrara Pro 5: *Daz3d.com*
Digital Film Tools Composite Suite and zMatte: *DigitalFilmTools.com*
dvGarage dvMatte Pro: *dvgarage.com*
e-on Vue: *eon.com*
The Foundry Keylight: *TheFoundry.co.uk*
Imagineer Systems Mocha and MochaAE: *ImagineerSystems.com*
Maxon Cinema 4D: *Maxon.net*
NewTek Lightwave: *Newtek.com*
Oak Street Software vKey2: *OakStreetSoftware.com*
Red Giant Magic Bullet Looks and Frames, Primatte Keyer Pro, Key Correct Pro: *RedGiantSoftware.com*
RE:Vision Effects FieldsKit, DE:Noise, ReelSmart Motion Blur, Twixtor Pro: *Revisionfx.com*

Save 5% at Toolfarm.com

As a thank you for purchasing this book, *Toolfarm.com* is offering a 5% discount on any item in the store. Use the coupon code in the checkout.
Coupon Code: GreenScreen

Training/Other Resources

DV Rebel's Guide by Stu Maschwitz: *rebelsguide.com*
FILMdyne: *FILMdyne.com*
Lynda: *Lynda.com*
Maxon Cineversity: *cineversity.com*
MicroFilmmaker Magazine: *Microfilmmaker.com*
Toolfarm: *Toolfarm.com*
istockphoto.com

GLOSSARY

24fps – Twenty-four frames per second is the speed that traditional film cameras record footage.

24P – Twenty-four progressive frames per second; this is the digital equivalent of the 24fps that film cameras shoot at.

3200K – The industry-standard Kelvin color rating for indoor lighting. 3200K emits a rather orange light.

35mm Lens Adapter – A special device that allows 35mm lenses to be used with a DV, HDV, or HD camera to create depth of field, angle of view, and focus typically found in 35mm film cameras.

3D Backgrounds – CGI background plates that are created in a 3D program such as Lightwave, 3D Studio Max, Cinema 4D, etc.

4:1:1 – The color sampling used in SD compression in most DV cameras. The first "4" refers to 4 luminance samples being taken over the range of 4 pixels. The "1" after that refers to 1 of 4 color samples being recorded over the range of 4 pixels in the first line of pixels. The "1" after that refers to 1 out of 4 color samples being recorded over the range of 4 pixels in the second line of pixels. The pattern is then repeated for the entire image.

4:2:0 – The color sampling used in the MPEG-2 compression used in most DV cameras, as well as the native compression used in PAL cameras. The first "4" refers to 4 luminance samples being taken over the range of 4 pixels. The "2" after that refers to 2 out of 4 color samples being recorded over the range of 4 pixels in the first line of pixels. The "0" after that refers to 0 out of 4 color samples being recorded over the range of 4 pixels in the second line of pixels. The pattern is then repeated for the entire image.

4:2:2 – The color sampling used in HD compression in most HD cameras. The first "4" refers to 4 luminance samples being taken over the range of 4 pixels. The "2" after that refers to 2 out of 4 color samples being recorded over the range of 4 pixels in the first line of pixels. The "2" after that refers to 2 out of 4 color samples being recorded over the range of 4 pixels in the second line of pixels. The pattern is then repeated for the entire image.

4:4:4 – The color sampling used in low-compression or no-compression video cameras, as well as RAW image formats used by DSLR and REDCode cameras. The first "4" refers to 4 luminance samples being taken over the range of 4 pixels. The "4" after that refers to 4 out of 4 color samples being recorded over the range of 4 pixels in the first line of pixels. The "4" after that refers to 4 out of 4 color samples being recorded over the range of 4 pixels in the second line of pixels. The pattern is then repeated for the entire image.

5600K – The industry-standard Kelvin color rating for outdoor or sunlight lighting. 5200K emits a rather blue light.

Alpha Channel – An alpha channel is a special type of channel used in graphics and 3D software to show an area in the image that is supposed to be transparent. Images and footage with an embedded alpha channel can be ported to other applications while retaining transparency as long as the other application supports alpha channels. Like a mask, the darkest area of an alpha channel is most transparent, white areas are opaque, and shades of gray represent varying levels of transparency.

Aperture – the size of the opening in the lens that determines the amount of light that falls onto the camera's sensor. The aperture is measured in "f-stops" or "f-numbers" (see also **F-Stops**).

AVI – AVI stands for Audio Video Interleave. It is a special case of the RIFF (Resource Interchange File Format). AVI is defined by Microsoft. AVI is the most common format for audio/video data on the PC. AVI is an example of a de facto standard.

Background Plate – The background that you'll be compositing your greenscreen footage into.

Backlight – sometimes referred to as a kicker, this light provides subtle illumination to the back of the head and provides better outline definition to the subject.

Bluescreen – A process whereby actors work in front of an evenly lit, monochromatic blue background. The background is then replaced in post-production by chromakeying, allowing other footage or computer-generated images to form the background imagery. This term is used to refer to the actual monochromatic blue background used for this type of work.

CGI – Computer-Generated Image, which refers to the use of computer graphics to create or enhance special effects.

Chroma – Chromanance, or color data.

Chromakey – A technique for mixing two images or frames together, in which a color (or a small color range) from one image is removed (or made transparent), revealing another image behind it (also known as **Color Key**).

Clean Plate – A shot of a greenscreen frame without the subject in the frame.

Codec – An abbreviation of "compressor-decompressor," a codec is a device or program capable of encoding and/or decoding a digital data stream or signal.

Color Grading – The process of correcting, changing, and enhancing the color of footage in postproduction.

Color Key – Also called Chromakey, this is a technique for mixing two images or frames together, in which a color (or a small color range) from one image is removed (or made transparent), revealing another image behind it.

Color Temperature – Term that describes the color of light sources; literally, the temperature at which a black body emits enough radiant energy to evoke a color equivalent to that coming from a given light source. Measured by degrees Kelvin, a high color temperature corresponds to bluer light, a low color temperature to yellow light. The color temperature of daylight is about 5500K to 5600K.

Composite – The combination of visual elements from separate sources into single images (or sequences of images), often to create the illusion that all those elements are parts of the same scene. Examples might be incorporating rendered 3D images (CGI) into filmed material, or extracting elements shot in front of blue/greenscreen. Today most compositing is achieved through digital image manipulation.

Compression – The process by which large video or image files are squeezed into smaller files to make them easier to store and quicker to transfer. There are two main types of compression: lossless and lossy. Lossless compression provides the highest-quality images by getting rid of none of the information that is recorded, making lossless compression images huge in size. Lossy compression provides lower-quality images because it gets rid of varying amounts of information to keep file sizes small. For video, virtually all recording is some form of lossy due to the sheer size constraints of truly uncompressed video. However, some forms of lossy recording have very little loss, like that used to create RAW and REDCode RAW. Compression formats that have much more compression are: HD, HDV, and DV.

Cyc Light – Long housings typically containing multiple lamps arranged along the length of the instrument and emitting light perpendicular to its length. These housings are often hinged to allow the lights to form a curve that can emit an even light across a cyclorama or other background.

Cyclorama – A large curtain or wall, usually concave, hung or placed at the rear of a stage. In greenscreen, this refers to a constructed greenscreen stage that has gently concave curves so that shadows don't get caught in any hard edges or corners.

Deartifact – To remove noise and compression damage from an image or video.

Despill – Suppression of light spill on your foreground object.

Diffuse Light – Light that is random in direction due to the fact that it has been passed through some sort of diffusion material that scatters it. Because this type of light is soft in nature, it tends to be much more flattering on faces than directional light. This type of light is also more uniform than directional light, so it is often used to illuminate things that need very uniform lighting, like greenscreens and bluescreens.

Diffusion – The transmission of light through a translucent material that causes the light to become scattered. This is also used to refer to the type of cloth used in a soft box or hung in flags in front of a light to diffuse the light's beam.

Digital Matte Painting – A matte painting that has been created in a computer environment in either 2D or 3D. Because it's much easier to superimpose digital backgrounds in greenscreen, this is used much more often than a traditional matte painting.

Directional Light – Lighting that originates from a dominant direction and provides shadow-casting illumination on an object or talent. Sunlight is a naturally occurring form of this light, while an artificially created key light would be another type.

DSLR – Digital Single Lens Reflex. A digital still image camera that uses a single lens reflex (SLR) mechanism. Most professional cameras have always been single lens reflex cameras, although in the past these were analog film cameras, rather than digital cameras.

DV – Digital Video. While DV can be used to refer to any camera that records to a DV tape, which includes Standard-Definition (SD) NTSC video cameras, PAL video cameras, and High-Definition Video (HDV), it is most commonly used to refer to SD NTSC video. The color sampling on SD DV footage is 4:1:1.

Fill Light – A type of light used to reduce the contrast of a scene and to provide some illumination for the areas of the image that are in shadow. Most lighting setups will place the fill light at a 90° angle to the key light (in relation to the subject).

Foreground Plate – The footage of your subject or talent shot in front of a greenscreen backdrop.

Flat Lighting – Low-contrast lighting that provides little or no shadowing. Often accomplished by axis lighting, where a light is put directly in front of the talent and as close to the camera's line of sight as possible to decrease shadows.

Fluorescent – A type of gas discharge lamp. While available in special screw-in bulbs, the most common types of these lights are available in glass tubes that have electrodes at the end of each bulb. The tube is normally filled with argon and some mercury. As current is applied at the electrodes, the mercury is vaporized by the argon gas. The mercury produces an ultraviolet emission. This then strikes the side of the tube, which is coated with a phosphor. The phosphor then transforms the ultraviolet to visible light. Unless specially treated, fluorescent lamps emit a dominant green hue that is not very suitable for a balanced light source — although such untreated bulbs can be very helpful for illuminating a greenscreen. When using fluorescent tubes, be sure to place them in a balanced ballast, as the discharge produced in an unbalanced ballast creates a non-uniform light that is easily detected as a 60-cycle flicker when playing images back from a high-speed motion analyzer.

Fresnel – A focusable spotlight used in film, television, and theater lighting, which can be adjusted via a knob on the back of the light from "spot" for a narrowly focused beam, to "flood" for a wider beam. Named after its inventor, French physicist Augustin-Jean Fresnel, this type of focusable lighting instrument is called a Fresnel because it features a Fresnel Lens, a glass lens with concentric ripples that are visible on the front of the light, casting soft, even illumination across the light's beam.

F-Stop – A measure of aperture in a lens or a camera, the f-stop is calculated by dividing the diameter of the aperture by the focal length of the lens. So a 50mm aperture on a lens with a focal length of 200mm would have an f-stop of $1/4$ — generally written as f4, F4, or 1:4. Because f-stops are essentially fractions, higher f-stops mean smaller apertures and thus less light hitting the sensor.

Gel – A thin, tinted plastic-like sheet placed over a light to change the color of the projected light.

Greenscreen – A newer technique similar to bluescreen but utilizing a green key background. Research showed that substantially better results could be gained by filming on green instead of blue with digital equipment, as digital recording methods are more sensitive to separating green from other (foreground) colors. This term is also used to refer to the actual monochromatic green background used for this type of work.

Halogen – A type of tungsten light. Halogen is a hotter lamp than many other tungsten lights because the bulb must heat a regenerative tungsten filament.

HD – High-Definition; currently used to refer to footage that is between 1080 and 1920 pixels in width; color sampling for HD is most commonly 4:2:2.

HDV – High-Definition Video; currently used to refer to a format that is between 1080 and 1920 pixels in width, uses MPEG-2 compression for video, compresses the audio to an MPEG audio codec, and has color sampling that is 4:2:0.

HMI – The most common form of arc discharge lamp. As current is passed through the HMI electrodes, an arc is generated and the gas in the lamp is excited to a light-emitting state. The spectrum of light emitted includes visible as well as ultraviolet rays. This light source typically has a UV filter to block harmful emissions. The HMI light is a balanced light source. It generates an intense white light. If a switching ballast is used with the HMI, it produces a uniform light with very low flicker. Other types of ballast are not as well regulated.

In-Camera Sharpening – An artificial sharpening of images inside the camera to create sharper images and reduce the likelihood of being out of focus. Unfortunately, this technique tends to create artifacts and other negative things in the image that are almost impossible to get rid of after the fact. It is not advised for bluescreen or greenscreen production.

Incandescent – Also referred to as tungsten, this is a type of light whose color temperature is 3200K. One of the most popular types of incandescent lamps are halogen lamps.

IRE – Institute of Radio Engineers. A way to measure video level, in which a unit is equal to 1/140 of the peak-to-peak amplitude of the video signal, which is typically 1 volt.

Interlace – To illuminate a screen by displaying all odd lines in the frame first and then all even lines. Interlacing uses half-frames per second (fields per second) rather than full frames per second. The interlace method was developed for TV broadcasting because the allotted bandwidth for TV channels, defined more than a half century ago, was not sufficient to transmit 60 full frames per second. Interlacing with 60 half-frames was visually better for moving images than 30 non-interlaced full frames.

Inverse Square Law – The scientific law that states that light doesn't drop off at a constant rate, but at the square of the distance it is moved from the subject.

Keyer – Software or mechanical device that allows you to remove the greenscreen or bluescreen behind your subject so that the background plate can show through.

Keyhole – The area of transparency in the foreground plate that occurs once a matte has been cut out via keying.

Key Light – A type of directional light, this is the photographic term for the main (and most powerful) light source, which can cause predominant shadows.

Kelvin – Named for Lord Kelvin, this is the official measure of color temperature (see also **Color Temperature**).

Knock Out – Slang term for a matte.

LED – Light-emitting diodes. Small, electronic components that let electricity pass in only one direction and emit visible light when electricity is applied, much like a light bulb. Because they need very little energy, LED lights are much cheaper to use than other types of lights and can last between 10,000 and 500,000 hours. Additionally, they can often be configured to change their light color when desired, which can make them very useful for greenscreen and bluescreen lighting.

Light Meter – A device used to measure the amount of light hitting a subject or background so that proper exposure can be accomplished.

Light Wrap – An area that wraps around the edges of your foreground image and brings some of the background colors into the foreground. This helps to make the edges blend better and helps make your foreground image appear more like it belongs in the shot.

Luma – Luminance, or brightness data.

Luma Keying – A way to remove a background using brightness, rather than color. Usually done with either pure white or pure black backgrounds.

Mask – A single channel layer used to define transparency or to cause a program to exclude an area in an image. While a chroma matte is a type of mask, most people use the term "mask" to refer to a hand "drawn" matte that excludes things from the image (i.e., a garbage matte).

Matte – A single channel layer that defines transparency and opacity on another image. In greenscreen, the matte would be created when the color green is chosen in the keyer and all areas of green in the foreground image become the matte. While a matte is a form of mask, people usually use the term "matte" when referring to keying and compositing, especially for chroma mattes.

Matte Choker – A tool that allows you to tighten or loosen your matte, usually pixel by pixel.

Matte Painting – A traditional photographic technique whereby artwork — usually on glass — from a matte artist is combined with live action. Digital matte painting is much more common in the modern era because of the sheer cost and technical difficulties of creating paintings on glass for films.

Motion Blur – The tendency of fast-moving objects to blur when they are captured on film or video. Shutter speed can have a lot to do with this.

Motion Capture – An animation technique in which the actions of an animated object are derived automatically from the motion of a real-world actor or object.

Motion Mattes – The term used to describe a matte that changes size and coverage frame by frame. Keyed greenscreen and bluescreen footage and 3D animations using an alpha channel all have motion mattes.

MultiPass Image – A 3D image that has multiple layers of information recorded from the 3D program that created it, which include things like 3D depth maps, camera information, lighting maps, and reflection maps. When used with compositing programs like Shake or After Effects, this information allows much more immersive compositing between keyed actors and 3D backgrounds and objects.

NTSC – National Television Standards Committee. The color system used in the United States and North America. The field rate for NTSC is 60Hz with 525 lines per screen and the subcarrier transmission method is a straight phase- and amplitude-modulation system for chroma, with a color sampling of 4:1:1.

PAL – Phase Alternation Line. This is the LockTV color system used everywhere in Europe except France. The field rate for PAL is 50Hz with 625 lines per screen. PAL uses a similar transmission method as NTSC, but with the color information switched 180 degrees on alternate scan lines, it has color sampling of 4:2:0.

Plug-in – A program that expands the ability of a host application but cannot be used on its own.

Progressive Scan – Illuminating a screen by displaying lines sequentially from top to bottom; also called non-interlaced. All modern computer display systems and many digital TV (DTV) formats support progressive scan. For example, 720p is an HDTV format that displays 720 lines of progressive scan signal.

Public Domain – Images, art, footage, music, or other created material that is not copyrighted. This refers both to things whose copyright has lapsed and to things that never had a copyright in the first place.

Pulling a Matte (or Pulling a Key) – Removing the greenscreen from your foreground plate to make that area transparent.

QuickTime – An image/video framework developed by Apple Computer to handle images, text, video, animation, music, and panoramic images. This is the dominant video type supported by Mac computers and their software.

RAID – Redundant Array of Independent Disks. RAID (originally "redundant array of inexpensive disks") is a way of storing the same data in different places (thus, redundantly) on multiple hard disks. Many RAID setups can keep running after a hard drive crashes and, once a new hard drive replaces the crashed one, completely rebuild all the information from the crashed drive.

RAW – A "raw," or unprocessed, digital image. Utilized heavily by DSLR cameras and by digital cinema cameras like the RED One, these extremely low-compression images are designed to retain as much of the original recorded information as possible for high-quality postproduction and effects work. Of course, their extremely high quality renders them extremely large, so they take up a lot of space and bandwidth. There are a number of different file extensions for this type of file, created by companies like Nikon, Canon, and RED.

REDCode RAW – A variable bitrate wavelet codec that allows raw sensor data at resolutions of up to 4096x2304 to be compressed sufficiently for practical on-camera recording. Currently two variants are offered, one with a maximum data rate of 28MB/s (224 megabits), and one with a maximum data rate of 36 MB/s (288 megabits). Compared with the uncompressed data captured by the sensor, these bitrates represent compression ratios of about 12:1 and 9:1, respectively.

Rendering – Referring to 3D programs, special effects programs, and editing programs, this is the final process of creating the actual 2D image or animation from the prepared scene or sequence.

Rotoscoping – The rotated projection of a sequence of photographed or CGI action image frames so that the artist can trace from the frame or create an image to superimpose on it. It can be thought of as essentially "painting on video" or "painting on film."

RPF – Rich Pixel Format. A type of picture that allows 3D programs to record 3D information like camera depth, reflection information, and other useful data.

SD – Standard Definition. Often used to refer to the NTSC size of 720 pixels wide by 480 pixels wide that was the most commonly used format in the U.S. until 2009. Color sampling in the NTSC convention is 4:1:1.

Shutter Speed – How fast a camera's shutter opens and closes. This determines how much light is recorded against the camera's optical sensors in each recorded frame of film or video. Slower shutter speed lets in more light but tends to yield a greater chance of blurring, while higher shutter speed lets in less light but has much more precise images.

Soft Box – A reflective enclosure that surrounds a light and bounces all light rays toward a single sheet of diffusion at the front of the enclosure. This creates a soft, nondirectional light, as opposed to a hard, directional one.

Spill – Colored light reflected from a background onto your talent.

Spill Algorithm – A special process built into most keyers that helps reduce or eliminate spill from your subject.

Stock Backgrounds – Backgrounds that are made available, royalty-free, for a set price for use in films and television productions.

Stop-Motion Animation – A form of animation in which objects are filmed frame by frame and altered slightly between each frame.

Subject – A term for whoever or whatever the focus of the camera is. Most often, the subject is the same thing as the "talent."

Talent – A general, informal term for actors (and possibly extras).

Timeline – A linear representation of items in your video sequence that displays the duration and order of footage, effect, and other elements.

Tracking Dots (or Tracking Marks) – Dots or crosses put on a greenscreen to allow moving camera shots to be tracked in postproduction and for backgrounds to move at a pace and manner that matches the camera movement.

Tracking Shot – In greenscreen, a shot that uses a moving camera and tracking dots on the greenscreen. In post, tracking or "match moving" programs are used to track these dots and then replace the greenscreen with a moving background plate that matches the pace and behavior of the camera.

Tungsten – Also referred to as incandescent, named according to the type of metal used in the filament (tungsten steel), this is a type of light whose color temperature is 3200K. One of the most popular types of tungsten lamps are halogen lamps.

Up Conversion or Up Rezing – Increasing the resolution of video from Standard-Definition to High-Definition.

Virtual Set – A computer-generated set designed to create a virtual reality around the real-world items and actors filmed in a greenscreen studio.

White Balance – A function for giving digital still and video cameras a reference point for white in order to render all the other colors of the spectrum naturally.

Zebra – A camera setting that allows you to visually see when you're over-exposing parts of your shot by putting diagonal lines into highlights in the viewfinder.

ABOUT THE AUTHORS

Jeremy Hanke is the editor-in-chief of *MicroFilmmaker* Magazine. He founded *MicroFilmmaker* Magazine in 2005 to help low-budget filmmakers make better films through traditional means like tips, articles, training tutorials, and reviews, but also by less common means like critiquing new films as they are created by both local and international filmmakers. In addition to helping low-budget filmmakers make better films, Jeremy has been able to use the magazine to connect filmmakers to indie musicians, scriptwriters, comics creators, financiers, distributors, and other groups that can help each other. *MicroFilmmaker* Magazine's approach has been so revolutionary that it's attracted filmmakers from every continent on the globe, including Antarctica.

When he's not editing the magazine, Jeremy works busily on films for his production firm, Viking Productions. He's directed two feature-length films, co-directed a 30-minute medium-short film, directed half a dozen short films, and produced multiple short films for aspiring filmmakers from underprivileged environments.

During his free time, he devours fantasy novels from the likes of Stephen R. Donaldson and Terry Brooks, plays Texas Hold 'em with his wife, Kari, and teaches Shudokan karate to his foster son, Richie.

Michele Yamazaki is the VP of Marketing & Web Development Czarina for *Toolfarm.com*, a value-added reseller of plug-ins and software. At Toolfarm, she juggles many roles, including developing content and training and answering support questions. She has demoed plug-ins for Apple, Boris FX, Red Giant, and other companies at NAB. In addition, she freelances and has spoken and taught at many user groups, schools, and conferences, including the Chicago Motion Graphics Festival. She is currently on the board of her local chapter of MCA-I and co-chairs the West Michigan Animation & Effects User Group, which she launched in 2002.

Michele was previously a visual effects and motion graphics artist at Postworks, a post house in Michigan. She was a contributing author of *After Effects @ Work*, published by Focal Press in 2006. She just wrapped up a four-year stint teaching After Effects at Kendall College of Art and Design.

She spends her spare time with her husband and daughter, Lily. She is an amateur chef, an aspiring screenwriter, a wannabe jet setter, and is involved with a local organic farm, trading Web skills for vegetables. She is a huge indie music connoisseur and recently launched *MaxBumps.net*, a music site for fans and artists. And, no, she's not Japanese.

SPECIAL EFFECTS
HOW TO CREATE A HOLLYWOOD FILM LOOK ON A HOME STUDIO BUDGET

MICHAEL SLONE

With advances in technology today, almost anyone can make a movie. If you have the passion, time, and a little money, you can turn your dreams into a big-screen experience. But you need more than technology alone to create something that people will want to see. This full color, comprehensive guide provides the tools to give your movie a Hollywood look — adding visual sizzle and eye-candy that can make a major difference in your film's future. This book includes:

· Step-by-step instructions on creating a wider variety of basic and advanced special effects techniques that will enhance your film or video project.
· Tips on how to work smart, play safe, and create interesting special effects that will help your film or video get noticed in film festivals, on YouTube, or on MySpace.
· Insider information from professional and Emmy®Award-winning special effects artists who have worked on such movies and shows as *Star Trek: Voyager*, *Sleepers*, *Contact*, *War of the Worlds*, *Lost*, *Alias*, and *Star Wars*.

"*This book is a great general purpose resource of practical and visual effects for the beginning filmmaker.*"
> – Eric Chauvin, Visual Effects Artist, *The Empire Strikes Back, War of the Worlds, Lost, Alias, The X-files*

"*This book shows how easy it can be to make Hollywood-style effects. If you're looking to increase the production value of your independent films or even your home movies, this is the book for you.*"
> – Per Holmes, Award-Winning Music Producer and Music Video Director

"*This book is a tremendous resource for all filmmakers. It contains so much information, you'll constantly be going back for more.*"
> – Andrew Kramer, Visual Effects Artist, Teacher, and Consultant

MICHAEL SLONE has been an independent filmmaker for over 12 years and has worked on small independent movies, as well as being a part of the major motion picture industry. With experience as a writer, director, cinematographer, and special effects coordinator, Slone created Studio 7 Productions *www.studio7movies.com* to help educate and support future filmmakers.

$31.95 · 260 PAGES · FULL COLOR · ORDER NUMBER 67RLS · ISBN: 9781932907261

THE WRITER'S JOURNEY
3RD EDITION

MYTHIC STRUCTURE FOR WRITERS

CHRISTOPHER VOGLER

BEST SELLER
OVER 170,000 COPIES SOLD!

See why this book has become an international best seller and a true classic. *The Writer's Journey* explores the powerful relationship between mythology and storytelling in a clear, concise style that's made it required reading for movie executives, screenwriters, playwrights, scholars, and fans of pop culture all over the world.

Both fiction and nonfiction writers will discover a set of useful myth-inspired storytelling paradigms (i.e., "The Hero's Journey") and step-by-step guidelines to plot and character development. Based on the work of Joseph Campbell, *The Writer's Journey* is a must for all writers interested in further developing their craft.

The updated and revised third edition provides new insights and observations from Vogler's ongoing work on mythology's influence on stories, movies, and man himself.

"This book is like having the smartest person in the story meeting come home with you and whisper what to do in your ear as you write a screenplay. Insight for insight, step for step, Chris Vogler takes us through the process of connecting theme to story and making a script come alive."
> - Lynda Obst, Producer, *Sleepless in Seattle, How to Lose a Guy in 10 Days;* Author, *Hello, He Lied*

"This is a book about the stories we write, and perhaps more importantly, the stories we live. It is the most influential work I have yet encountered on the art, nature, and the very purpose of storytelling."
> - Bruce Joel Rubin, Screenwriter, *Stuart Little 2, Deep Impact, Ghost, Jacob's Ladder*

CHRISTOPHER VOGLER is a veteran story consultant for major Hollywood film companies and a respected teacher of filmmakers and writers around the globe. He has influenced the stories of movies from *The Lion King* to *Fight Club* to *The Thin Red Line* and most recently wrote the first installment of *Ravenskull*, a Japanese-style manga or graphic novel. He is the executive producer of the feature film *P.S. Your Cat is Dead* and writer of the animated feature *Jester Till*.

$26.95 · 300 PAGES · ORDER NUMBER 76RLS · ISBN: 193290736x

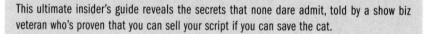

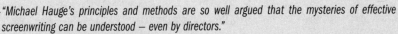

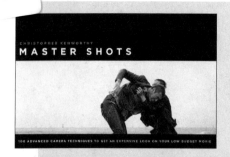

MASTER SHOTS
100 ADVANCED CAMERA TECHNIQUES TO GET AN EXPENSIVE LOOK ON YOUR LOW BUDGET MOVIE

CHRISTOPHER KENWORTHY

Master Shots gives filmmakers the techniques they need to execute complex, original shots on any budget. By using powerful master shots and well-executed moves, directors can develop a strong style and stand out from the crowd. Most low-budget movies look low-budget, because the director is forced to compromise at the last minute. *Master Shots* gives you so many powerful techniques that you'll be able to respond, even under pressure, and create knock-out shots. Even when the clock is ticking and the light is fading, the techniques in this book can rescue your film, and make every shot look like it cost a fortune.

Each technique is illustrated with samples from great feature films and computer-generated diagrams for absolute clarity.

Use the secrets of the master directors to give your film the look and feel of a multi-million-dollar movie. The set-ups, moves and methods of the greats are there for the taking, whatever your budget.

"*Master Shots gives every filmmaker out there the blow-by-blow setup required to pull off even the most difficult of setups found from indies to the big Hollywood blockbusters. It's like getting all of the magician's tricks in one book.*"
— Devin Watson, Producer, *The Cursed*

"*Though one needs to choose any addition to a film book library carefully, what with the current plethora of volumes on cinema,* Master Shots *is an essential addition to any worthwhile collection.*"
— Scott Essman, Publisher, *Directed By* Magazine

"*Christopher Kenworthy's book gives you a basic, no holds barred, no shot forgotten look at how films are made from the camera point of view. For anyone with a desire to understand how film is constructed — this book is for you.*"
— Matthew Terry, Screenwriter/Director, Columnist
www.hollywoodlitsales.com

Since 2000, CHRISTOPHER KENWORTHY has written, produced, and directed drama and comedy programs, along with many hours of commercial video, tv pilots, music videos, experimental projects, and short films. He's also produced and directed over 300 visual FX shots. In 2006 he directed the web-based Australian UFO Wave, which attracted many millions of viewers. Upcoming films for Kenworthy include *The Sickness* (2009) and *Glimpse* (2011).

$24.95 · 240 PAGES · ORDER NUMBER 91RLS · ISBN: 9781932907513